LIVING ON

EXMOOR

by

Hope L. Bourne

ILLUSTRATED
BY THE
AUTHOR

EXMOOR BOOKS

First published by Galley Press 1963
Second, revised edition 1991. Reprinted 2002
Third edition 2010. Revised 2014

British Library Cataloguing-in-Publication Data
A CIP record for this title is available from the British Library

ISBN 978 0 86183 449 5

EXMOOR BOOKS
Exmoor Books is a Partnership Between
Halsgrove and the Exmoor National Park

Halsgrove House,
Ryelands Business Park,
Bagley Road, Wellington, Somerset TA21 9PZ
Tel: 01823 653777   Fax: 01823 216796
email: sales@halsgrove.com

Part of the Halsgrove group of companies
Information on all Halsgrove titles is available at:
www.halsgrove.com

Printed and bound in China
by Everbest Printing Co Ltd

Contents

Illustrations

Foreword

HOPE BOURNE was a woman of many apparent contradictions. Physically tiny, she spent years undertaking sometimes backbreaking farm work. For much of her life she immersed herself in Exmoor, its landscape and its people, yet she undertook major expeditions to both Canada and Australia. She lived alone and apart for decades, yet she regularly sent and received over a hundred Christmas cards from friends at home and abroad. Of little formal education, save what she was taught by her widowed schoolmistress mother, she nevertheless developed a lapidary prose style that for many placed her among the top half dozen writers about the countryside and country ways.

It was in 1962 that Hope Bourne submitted the manuscript of what was her first and probably finest book, *Living on Exmoor*, to Dent and Co. She despatched it in her customary form – hand written in pencil. The publisher, recognising its quality, returned it fully typed and it duly appeared in print in 1963. Into the book Hope distilled much of her close understanding of the rhythm of the rural year, illustrated with her own exquisite pen and ink and pencil drawings. The book immediately established Hope Bourne's fame and led to three further books over the next thirty years – *A Little History of Exmoor, Wild Harvest* and *A Moorland Year.* There were others on which Hope continued to work, invariably drafted in pencil although as a concession to posterity she did usually make a fair copy in ballpoint pen.

That any of these works could be completed or indeed survived at all was in itself something of a minor miracle. Although Hope had been born in Oxford in 1918, much of her childhood was spent near Hartland, one of the remotest parts of Devon, where her mother was the headmistress of a village school. As an asthmatic Hope remained at home, moving with her mother to the Cotswolds in 1939. Hope was in her thirties when her mother died and she found herself with no home, no qualifications and little money. Thereupon she decided to return to the South West and become self-sufficient, working on farms to earn a little money and to grow or shoot what she needed to eat. A succession of basic Exmoor cottages gave way in the 1970s and 1980s to an old caravan at Ferny Ball near Withypool, parked up in a ruined farmstead where Hope was allowed to stay in return for keeping an eye on the farmer's livestock. Damp and mouse damage were ever-present threats to the survival of Hope's writings and drawings. But she persevered and both her work and her "primitive" lifestyle attracted increasing attention. Television found her in the late 1970s and three documentaries in succeeding decades chronicled her almost hunter-gatherer existence and her (usually forthright) opinions – exalting of country people and their sports, utterly damning of city values and bureaucrats. She became a "personality" but never lost her sense of vocation as a writer. It was through her pen that she had real influence and how she touched the hearts of others most profoundly. Her books sum up better than any, deep rural life in the late twentieth century when technology, mass media and the tentacles of urban living had made inevitable inroads, but the essence of lives tied to the land and governed by the seasons was still remarkably as it had been for hundreds of years.

Despite her delicacy in youth and hard life, Hope Bourne's petite frame bore her into her tenth decade. Although recurrent asthma forced her to leave Ferny Ball for a little house in Withypool, she took her beloved bantams with her and she still persisted in sleeping beside the fire every night rather than resorting to anything as mundane as a bed. Here it was that she died just a few days short of her 92nd birthday, and in Withypool that a churchful of friends, neighbours and admirers came to remember a woman who loved the English countryside and its traditions with a passion and Exmoor most fiercely of all.

Introduction
to the Second Edition

SINCE I wrote this little book some twenty eight years ago much
has changed.

Half the wild land I knew has disappeared under the plough,
(the official estimate is 20 to 25%, but remembering all the steep
cleeves, small woodlands and tangled odd corners now gone, I still
say half). New wire fences have marched across open moorland,
modern machinery has torn the sides of combes which an older
pattern of farming had left to themselves. Yearly both heather and
bent-and-bracken moor have diminished.

Wilderness does not really exist now. Not only do new fences so
often bar the old freedom to be an explorer, but where accepted
paths prevail they are mapped and way-marked and trampled
plain. There is no adventure walking on the moor nowadays.

The traditional farming has all but disappeared too. New
breeds of livestock have replaced the old, the tractor has ousted the
horse, no corn is grown and silage-making tends more and more to
take the place of haymaking. The modern shepherd is more likely
to drive a Land Rover than to ride a pony. Big modern general-
purpose barns mark the landscape whilst the older buildings are
converted to other uses or just crumble away. Saddest of all, so
many small farms have ceased to exist as independent holdings,
their land being attached to the larger farms and their houses sold
away from them.

Nor are there any more small, simple, half-forgotten cottages
tucked away in the wilderness. Those that have not quite tumbled
down have been refurbished and modernized to serve mostly as
holiday cottages or second homes. Lanes have been tarmacked
and poles and wires march in lonely parts. And over so much of
the countryside the great beech fences which served as windbreaks
and were so much a part of the character of the land have been
shaved down to suburban-type hedges about featureless fields.

Yet, surprisingly, much remains. Across the great shoulders of
Dunkery the heather is still an unbroken sweep of summer purple,
whilst Cloutsham woods lie deep and mysterious in shadow below.
Other hills, too, Winsford and Withypool and Molland Moor,

remain heather-clad, and the five beautiful waters of the north—Weir, Chalk, Badgery, Farley and Hoaroak—are largely unspoilt. The valleys of the Barle and the Exe are lovely in almost all their reaches. The Chains still carry desolate bog.

The Red Deer flourish and the foxes are a pest. The huntsman's horn and the cry of the hounds still stir the blood on an autumn morning.

Buzzards still soar, the cuckoo calls in the valleys, there are bluebells in the woods and the gorse flares golden in the waste places. Ponies graze on the commons and shy wild things peer from the cover. So all is not lost.

H. L. B. Ferny Ball, 1990.

Preface

THIS WORK may perhaps best be called a book of days, for it consists for the most part of the memories of many days, as recorded in a journal, kept over a period of years, here extracted and pieced together to form the cycle of one year and to give— I hope—some picture of the nature and character of a loved land.

The descriptions of farm life are mostly taken from an interim period of a year or so between the selling of one house and the obtaining of another, during which time I lived on a friend's isolated hill farm. There is a good deal about hunting in most parts, for with five packs of hounds hunting the moor for a consecutive period of nearly ten months of the year, one is seldom out of sight or sound of the hunt at any time or place other than around midsummer. Of fishing there is nothing at all, since it is a sport and subject about which I remain completely ignorant despite a lifetime spent in country surroundings. Of folklore and superstition there is nothing either, for apart from an occasional vague reference to a certain place being 'haunted', I have heard no such tales first-hand in the past twenty years—the wireless and the 'telly' would seem to have put a final end to such things.

On looking back through the pages written, I am aware that there is a certain amount of repetition, both of expression of feeling and of general description, but I have preferred to leave it so, for the reason that most of the material remains just as written down at the time of happening, and thus spontaneous and directly descriptive of the thoughts and emotions then evoked. After all, these descriptions are of life lived, and are not intended as works of art or literature.

So may I dare to hope that what is written down in the following may perhaps be of interest to some of those others who, like myself, have loved the moor and all its farms and fields and hills, its changing seasons, its creatures and its deeper mysteries.

H. L. B.

February

A FEBRUARY afternoon. Under the leaden, rain-filled sky the moor lies desolate, wind-lashed, streaked and curdled still with snow, rolling in heaving undulations like the billows of a tideless sea, reaching up to dark skylines swallowed in grey cloud. Soaking bent and sodden rush, black dripping heather, bracken soaked to dark mahogany, and the icy white of snow a livid dappling in every hag and hollow. There is no life, no sound but the beating rain, no voice but that of the wind. It is loneliness and desolation, the western land as was in the beginning, storm swept and primeval. The wind blows over the dun-coloured bent and the squelching peat bogs, over the forlorn barrows sunk in mystery on the hills, over the long blue moorstone walls and down through the tattered, cowering beech and twisted thorn and into the combes where sallow and rowan coil about the rushing streams. The rain beats on the strange stones that stand knee deep in the wet black heather and on the dark low thickets of gorse, and drives splashing into the pools that lie at the feet of the lonely gateways and all the little quivering rills amongst the rushes.

Down from the moor, under the rim, lies the old farm, its fields sodden and dun-coloured, desolate in a winter world, its hedges stark and black above the long white seams of snow that lie as yet unmelted by the driving rain. The wet slate roofs and old stone walls of the farmstead huddle together in a knot of wind-battered beeches, house and barn and shippon close and tight in a hostile element. Its yards and gateways are all squelch and slush and splashing mud. Around the buildings the raw sou'wester seems to blow the rain in all directions at once, so that there is no shelter anywhere, dashing the wet into one's face from the eaves and gutters and tree branches, flinging it round all the corners and into every doorway, until one is soaked at every point. About the streaming yards the hens huddle miserably under the walls and in any partly sheltered angle, and at the gates the cattle crowd nearly hock deep in the liquid mud, hungry for the food and warmth of the shippons. Farther out the sheep gather together on the poached ground around the feeding troughs, expectant, while imperceptibly the day's light begins to fade and the chiller cold of evening takes hold on all things.

In the gathering dusk a small band of ponies comes down from the moor, emerged from the depths of some combe, and they look fearfully and longingly round the bend of the lane towards the farm. They are like wild creatures, with their wet reddish-brown bodies blending with the rough banks and trees of the lane and only their mealy noses showing up clearly in the fading light. They are so small and nervous, yet our cows, usually so pushful and domineering on their way home to food and milking, seem afraid to pass them.

Now it is evening. As the short day closes the windows of the farmhouse glow with orange light, beacons against the coming darkness. Now at last the day's work is done. Now is the time of the evening meal, and the gathering round the fire that blazes on the open hearth. The flames leap from the blazing beech logs, sending branched shadows dancing on the walls from the hanging stags' antlers. The dogs and cats clustered round the hearth stir lazily into more comfortable positions, and stretch themselves before the warmth, while the mounting wind rattles the doors and windows, shaking the latches and making the oil lamps flicker in the draught.

Here are warmth and light and comfort and food, and safety in the night. Yet even here one feels the presence of the moor. Though unseen, it is all around—pressing in on the little fields and lonely farm, a brooding presence, dominant and impelling, something dark, primeval, untamed, like a sleeping beast coiled all around.

Through many long winter nights past men of the moor have sat as we sit tonight with their dogs by the fire, listening to the wind and thinking of the many things around them—of their cattle and their sheep, of deer and foxes and hunting, of last year's crops and the spring that is to come. Time goes on and many things change, yet many things remain, and those that are elemental are timeless. But one grows drowsy by the fire. Soon it will be time for bed, and then even the moor and the farm and the storm will be forgotten until tomorrow morning.

§

A WEEK of snow, cold desolate February snow, covering everything with white, choking the gateways, filling the yards with slush, clogging the narrow lanes, softening to a floundering mess by day, chilling and freezing under the frosts of night, and making heavy work of all things about the farm.

Now a grey still morning, with a thick grey-white mist closing in, muffling and clammy, slowly turning the snow and the frosted ground to squelch and slush, and setting all the branches dripping.

Presently the mist lifts, and lifting shows the pale, washed

3

green of fields, and farther off the moor, all brown and purple-black, streaked and patched with white on the shoulders of all its combes. It seems an archaic land, brooding and far off in time, yet with a presence that seems to lift one's heart.

About mid afternoon there is a sudden stir among the farm dogs, and I hear the cry of the hounds. Then galloping hoofs, and the flash of a red coat—a swinging gate, and horsemen are galloping away hard across the Twelve-Acres. The sheep bunch in the corner and our dogs run wild. Louder, clearer, fierce and insistent, the cry of the hounds running hard! How the heart leaps! For a brief moment all cares are cast aside, and one is drawn back to the world of beasts and gods, back to the springs of life and desire. They seem for a moment not mortal hounds but spirits born of the dark, snow-splashed moor, hunting their prey from beyond the limits of man's world to the edges of some pagan kingdom.

Now they are swinging in a great arc, straight towards the farm. I drop my bucket and run for a view, all else forgotten. Nearer and nearer—and then suddenly I see them, streaming under the hedge of the second meadow. They sweep over the grass in a screaming wave, and then check. There is sudden silence, and they cast themselves back, trying all the hedge-banks. I scramble through a gap and stand by the little rill and watch them. They are no longer pied beasts, but brown—splashed and stained by the mud of a wet season to a dark dun colour. They cast hither and thither, trying very hard, but somehow they cannot recover the line. Somehow the fox has eluded them. At last there is a sound of hoofs, and the huntsman comes to their aid. He lifts them, and takes them on. I long to follow down into the tangled combes, but I have other things to do today, so must forgo it. The last I see of them is a red coat cantering down the old lane.

The afternoon slips back to the usual tenor of things. Presently the engine in the round-house begins to throb, and then the thresher in the barn to whine and rattle. I go to lend a hand for a while. The barn is full of noise and dust as the stack of last year's oat sheaves in the lower end is pulled apart and the sheaves forked up into the threshing-machine that is built against the wall. Dust and chaff fly everywhere, setting everyone coughing, and masses of straw pile up in the midst, faster than

4

anyone can move the stuff, and the dogs of course are all over the place in everybody's way, oblivious to the stabbing pitchforks and intent only on a passionate search for rats and mice. The threshing is for the benefit of the horses, for the cattle receive their quota of corn in the sheaf and so do the sheep when there is enough to spare for them as well. Though corn is a difficult crop in the hills—that is to say difficult to harvest—one is glad to have what one can, for the oats and their straw are good food for all beasts in hard weather, and, as the folk say, one misses the oaten sheaves when one hasn't got them.

Enough is done for a month or so, and somebody turns off the small engine at the back of the round-house. Our round-house is a peculiar building, preceding in date and purpose the invention of the petrol-driven engine. It is octagonal in actual form, some thirty odd feet in diameter, and was originally built for the housing of the horse-tackle by which the threshing-machine was then worked. I gather that the horse was attached in some way to some sort of circular gear, about which it walked in endless rounds, and that the power thus generated was transferred by a series of cogs and belts to the driving parts of the thresher.

Nowadays our round-house has long ago forgotten its original purpose, and serves mostly as an overflow department for its neighbour the barn, housing all the odd things that cannot find room there.

§

THE OLD farm sits low on the hill that lies under the moor. The sun of a bright spring-like morning shines on the low buildings grouped under the weather-beaten beeches, and on the fields that lie in a pale green chequerwork amongst the big hedges, and on the running streams and the tawny moor that laps beyond the hill. It touches the rough stone walls and the old slate roofs with golden light and gilds the heads of all the trees, and reaches with long fingers into the yards and into the depths of the shippons, and sets the splat sparkling like a shattered mirror. Birds twitter in the trees and hedges, and there is fresh green grass at the edge of the splat, and winter seems forgotten for a little while.

The farm seems to doze. It has known many such mornings, for it is one of the ancient farms of the moor, that has crouched here on the hill for many winters, for long centuries that reach back into the Middle Ages and beyond. Long ago, perhaps in the dim years of the thirteenth century, perhaps even before the Norman Conquest, some forgotten pioneer moved up from the lowland to the moor and set his hand upon the hill, and carved its first little fields out of the wastes of heather and bracken, and built its first buildings of thin grey stone. The farm tells no tales. It has no history as we know it, yet it has known much history. All that we know of it is that out of the dim and distant past there comes from time to time in ancient parish or Forest documents some mention of its name and a man's name, to tell us that a lonely farm sat on the lonely hill when kings made war in France and princes quarrelled for the English throne, when deer were royal beasts and pack-horses splashed in the muddy tracks.

The way to it is still by the narrow, twisting lane that is little more than a track, sunk deep between the fields, scored down to the rock in places and slippery with mud in most parts. Its water supply is still the splat, the little stream that runs down from the moor, guttered carefully through the intervening fields, to emerge at last here by the outer yard. Here the bright sparkling water, running along its little channel from the low, stone-slabbed tunnel in the last field bank, drops splashing over a step of stone—set long ago to facilitate the filling of a bucket—and then spills over into the laneway and across it, to continue its way through the yards and away down the lower fields beyond.

Here is the yard, worn to bed-rock and rutted by endless hoofs and centuries of rain, and house and barn and shippon and stable grouped close around the square—all facing inwards and presenting blank walls to the outer world. This is the oldest pattern of a hill farm, from which all other layouts are but adaptations or later alterings. Many times over, the buildings must have been built and rebuilt since the first foundations were set, yet the foundations themselves will not have changed, or at least only a very little. Even now many of the rough stone

6

walls must be very old. Seen from without, as one approaches uphill from the laneway, the farm still presents a fortress-like appearance with its blank walls broken only by very small, loop-hole openings. Here, as so often when approaching an ancient hill farm with its tight courtyard grouping and frowning outer aspect, one has almost the feeling of coming to a castle; and indeed it is possible that this impression is not wholly an illusion, and that defence may actually have been a consideration, for in olden times there was but little law in this wild and lonely country, and little restraint on violence when neighbour quarrelled with neighbour and only the power of a man's own hand defended his house and ricks.

The whitewashed face of the house shines brightly into the yard where the golden-brown muck-hills pile in heaps of accumulated fertility before the shippon doors. The house itself is plain and slate-roofed, only its big chimneys giving evidence of its greater age (once it was low and thatched, as were all ancient moorland farmhouses, but a generation ago it suffered a serious fire which necessitated the rebuilding of the upper parts). Shippon and barn and stable look at each other across the yard, sun-splashed with pools of shadow at their feet and hay-filled loft and tallet under their low roofs. The cow-shippon joins to the house, as is the ancient way, and from within come the chink and rattle of the cow-ties as the beasts toss their heads against the ashen stall-trees, impatient for their morning feed. They bawl occasionally, calling to their calves. A dog barks somewhere out of sight, and the horses stamp in the stable. In the open door of a loft a cat curls on the sill to drowse in the welcome sunlight. The scent of sweet hay mingles with the sour-sweet smell of the middens on the cobbles. A pair of pied wagtails flutter and run with some other small birds that search for seeds dropped from oat sheaves or hay bundles.

The sun makes patterns on the rough texture of the walls, on narrow ragwork and bolder rubble, warming the hints of brown and rose-pink under the grey surface, touching the splashes of yellow lichen to bright gold. Here in the stonework one can see the whole range of the Devonian rock that is the bone of the land. Textures of soft slate and hard dark sandstone, colours that run from blue-grey to rose-pink and deep plum colour. Those buildings which seem to be the oldest are all built of grey slaty shale laid in thin ragwork. This is the surface stone hereabouts, found as outcrop or loose clitter on the steep slopes of the combe beyond the farm. This would be the first stone to come to the hand of early builders, lying as it were for the taking. Other buildings, those which have obviously been added to the group in fairly recent times, are of a more massive sort of rock, a bold reddish sandstone that is set in rubble fashion. This stone represents a lower stratum, and although it also comes from this same hill, it has to be quarried for, and so brought to the surface. The old pits from which it was dug can still be seen in two of the fields not far away. So one can mark how the old farm has grown from the very ground on which it stands, as much as any tree about it.

The buildings themselves are very low and plain. The rough, intractable stone does not give much play to architecture. One small unpretentious building is noteworthy—the ash house. Once every farm had its ash-house. Here the rich ash from the peat that was burnt on the open hearth would be stored all the winter to be later drawn out and spread on the fields as a spring fertilizer. So valuable a manure was the peat ash that it was sometimes sold, I believe, to gardeners and others, who came long distances with carts to get it. One can still see, low at the foot of the little building, the small square opening once closed with a little wooden shutter through which the accumulated ash was drawn out each spring.

Between the buildings and the lapping fields is a small stoutly enclosed garden, and in this little high-banked garden behind the hay barn the sun is held as in an embrace. Here every branch, every stone in the bank, every blade of rough grass is clear cut and suffused as it were with a strange beauty. Snowdrops lift their white heads in little snowy drifts and clusters along the south-facing bank, and the hellebores open green cups at the foot. The fallow ground is decked with gold, the first flowers of the coltsfoot thrust up naked from the bare earth, answering the call of the spring to come. As to the hellebores, green faces in green ruffed necks, they are always the first flowers of the year here in the old garden. Probably they are naturalized, planted once by someone; but in parts of North-West Devon they are wild, and for me they are always the green heralds of spring.

I turn away down the lane and think of other things. The day slides on. Morning turns to afternoon, and afternoon to evening. It is dusk when I return to the farm. Now the buildings stand up dark to the sky, and there are orange lights in the house windows. A sickle moon shines above the roofs. There is a rustle of frost underfoot, and the coldness of night all around. The splat runs noisily in the stillness. Do ghosts move in the shadows? Perhaps. The farm is old enough, and so many loves and hates and hopes and fears must be bound up in it. But it is cold to stand about, and the warmth within beckons; so ghosts must keep company with themselves for another night.

§

AFTERNOON, and I stand in a neighbour's yard where Muscovy ducks splash at the water and red cattle laze in the sunny angles.

The ducks, like harlequins in their black and white and red, bob and waddle at the splat. Then suddenly disturbed at a stranger's notice or by some other thing, they spread their wings and rise, and plane down the yard in a splendid fantasy of flight and colour.

The red cattle stand silently in the winter sun, brooding, thinking whatever thoughts cattle do think betwixt food and sleep. Except for an occasional movement as one or the other shifts a little across the open yard that lies between house and barn, they might be great archaic figures carved from some dark red substance in another age. Huge white horns sweep up from big, deep-jowled heads like the horns of beasts in an ancient fresco, and rich crimped and curling hair covers the ponderous bodies. Here they stand, the red cattle of Devon in the yard that has known no other breed in all its long and patient history.

Behind the cattle a knot of tall beech trees rises from an old wide wall into which their roots are dug as fingers to hold themselves upright and so to reach upwards to the sky with spreading heads. The afternoon sun sculptures the massive trunks, turning them to pillars of silver-gold, and from them casts back hard blue shadows on to the walls and roof of the old plain grey barn.

On the opposing side of the yard, its face now in the shadow, stands the farmhouse and its shippons. An old house, possibly of the seventeenth century (indeed I am told that a stone dated '16—' used to be visible over one of the doors), slate-roofed and now cream washed, having a little garden before its front door, and the shippons joining to it at the south end. Here is the old order of things—house and shippon in one continuous block, with the door of the cow-shippon and the main house door opening side by side on to a wide sweep of gently sloping cobbles. Only the grey tractor under a lean-to roof marks this day and age.

Somewhere a door bangs and there is a momentary sound of footsteps. The cattle lift heads expectantly. Soon perhaps they will gain re-admittance to the low, dim, desirable shippons, replete with food and fresh bedding, and warm against the cold wet nights. As is the custom in the hills, all except the roughest bullocks are wintered in. The fine red cattle commonly lie in from December to April or the beginning of May, though in point of fact they are extremely hardy beasts, bred as they are to the wild wet climate of their native North Devon. I lean for a moment on the grassy edge of the bank, my feet on the plank that bridges the splat at the point where it disappears under the drain way and my face turned to the slight warmth of the February sun, and contemplate the standing cattle. They are the cattle of the west, the beasts of combe and hill and lonely farmstead, and I can remember the time when no other beasts were to be seen west of Taunton. Their long, white, wide-spreading horns seem to reach out to pierce through time, back through the generations of nameless farmers and a thousand farms, new-cut from moor and forest, through hidden years of fighting and raiding, back to the days when all beasts were wild, and cattle roamed in herds on the hill or browsed in the leafy bottoms and were a hunter's prey.

Though the earliest written references to the 'red cattle of Devon' date only from the Elizabethan period, there is no reason for doubting that our long-horned, red cattle are indigenous to the west. Wild cattle existed in most of Britain in prehistoric times in company with deer and wild horses, and it would seem most probable that some remnant of an ancient race drifted into the western peninsula in remote times, there to remain to be gradually tamed and domesticated by the hardy farmers of long ago. Indeed I recall having read somewhere that as late as the sixteenth century the farmers of the wilder parts of Cornwall kept their cattle in wild roaming herds, hunting them down at certain times for the purpose of slaughtering a number for meat. If this is so, then it must surely represent the survival of a tradition of regarding cattle as wild animals, rather than, as might seem, just plain bad husbandry.

The fine massive beef cattle that we see today—the famous Red Rubies of Devon—are as a type the product of several devoted breeders of the eighteenth century and early nineteenth century, notably the Quartleys of Molland and the Davys of Rose Ash. It is to the Quartleys, who came to farm at Molland in the eighteenth century, that we owe the first improvement of the native breed. For a hundred years or more they bred and developed the red cattle, until by 1850 the type was perfected by Francis Quartley, in recognition of whose work a presentation portrait was subscribed for in that year by many gentlemen and farmers. In 1851 John Tanner Davy began to compile the first herd book. The Davys had themselves been breeding fine cattle for at least 150 years prior to this and the stock of many another lesser farmer might be traced for nearly as far back, so it may thus be fairly said that the pure-bred Devon of today can show a pedigree that may go back through more than two hundred years of known ancestry to the ancient stock of the western land.

The Devon of today is a splendid beast, broad and deep and short-legged, bred for beef yet still giving plentiful milk—the best butter I know is made from the milk of these beef cows—and able to thrive on rough pasture. The hallmark of the race is still the rich red colour—ruby red in summer, but deepening to a dark mahogany in winter. The deep pendulous jowl, unlike that of any other breed and prominent even in the youngest calves, is another characteristic. A true Devon should have no white upon it save a tag to the tip of the tail, but the herd book does allow a single splash on the back part of the belly. The horns of a Devon cow, full grown, have, I think, the greatest spread of any present-day breed save the

Highland, and are a heritage perhaps from some primeval aurochs strain.

The excellence of the pure Devon has caused it to become known far beyond its native west in recent years, and today there are herds not only in other parts of Britain but also in Brazil, Jamaica, Kenya, South Africa, Australia, New Zealand and U.S.A. So have they spread like pioneers from the west, the home of the pioneers.

Once, long ago, the Devon cattle served another purpose as well as that of beef-and-milk beasts. I have somewhere in my possession an ox-shoe that was given me after having been unearthed in Exford during some drain-laying work. Teams of red oxen must once have worked in the fields and moved in the lanes, and a great sight such a team must have been, perhaps eight huge, red-bodied, deep-jowled beasts, moving slowly over a hilltop, their sweeping wax-white horns piercing the sky.

But the thin winter sun is losing its little power as the afternoon wanes, and it is cold standing by the water. Soon the beasts will return to the stuffy warmth of their shippons, and there will be milking, and then tea in the farmhouse kitchen where the lamplight shines on the long, laden table, and news and music from the radio on the window-sill.

It is time to go home. Already the sun is sinking in a great golden glow, and from afar off, as though from the courts of the setting sun, the notes of a blackbird come faint yet clear, like the spell of an enchanter. Then the sun slips beyond the rim and is gone.

§

THE LAST day of February. A morning grey and ominous, working up for rain on a rising wind. Across the moor a tractor crawls slowly on the rough track, laboriously towing the long baler in its wake, lurching and vibrating over the stones and ruts as it comes. Two fields in from the moor men are hurriedly stripping the thatch from the long low rick of last summer, in readiness for its coming. A worse day for the job could hardly happen.

Midday, and the wind risen to a howling gale. The sky all dark rolling cloud, splatters of rushing rain, and everything bitterly cold and wet. Under the hedge, in the space between it and the rick, the baler is drawn into position and set and wedged. The tractor starts to chug and throb, and the long red baler to clank, and the work begins.

I carry and stack. Luckily I am on the lea side of the rick— the wind is a wild sea gale, coming straight off the Atlantic. It is so strong one can hardly stand against it. It cuts and batters, it is raw with the rawness of the cold ocean. It whips through one's clothing with a numbing bite. I flatten myself back against the rick to try and get a bit of shelter. On the rick the man can hardly get the hay off and over, or even keep his footing. The hay flies from his fork like a battle-standard, ripping away in streamers, smothering everyone, choking the machinery, and decking the hedge in tawny tatters. Beyond the men and machinery the long line of the moor lies dark like the rim of an everlasting ocean, flinging cloud and storm over the farmland. Bursts of rain, now blowing level with the fields, sting like hail. At last we must stop, for it is not possible to continue any longer. I climb on the stack of sixty bales to wrestle with the sheet. It is like being a sailor at sea, face to face with the unfettered elements. I can hardly manage, with the rocking bales and the floundering, flying rick-sheet like a sail, and almost fall off. We struggle to stake the sheet with cord and pitchforks, but they pull out. Somehow we get it fixed after a fashion and head for home. The gate swings in the wind so that we can hardly shut it. The wind is like a demon. Oh, the blessed shelter of the lane!

All day long the wind increases until by nightfall all the land bends before the gale. The day dies under the heavy cloud with the darkness of a moonless night. The great beech hedges roar in the wind like the voice of a storm god. The noise is deafening. The only sound to rise above it is the clang of tin tearing loose on a shippon roof. There will be wreckage by the morning. The wind comes in great gusts, with the rhythm of the sea—sucking back, then striking with screaming, battering force like the blow of a great fist. The rain flies with the wind, driven in streaming torrents. The trees arch and bend in the bleakness, and torn branches fall to trip one in the darkness. Flying slates make

another hazard near the barn. What a night! Even the storm
lantern may blow out on a night like this. All things crouch for
shelter: the sheep close in tight to the banks, the ponies somewhere in the lowest bottoms of the combes. Lucky are all things,
man and beast, that lie under a roof tonight. Tomorrow is
another month, and truly March has come in well.

March

THE WINDS of March blow over the moor on a morning after a stormy night. Sudden squalls of rain alternate with bursts of scalding sunlight, and a myriad raindrops glitter from the dark heather and from every point of grass.

As I stand for a moment to watch the flying clouds, a small herd of ponies appears on the skyline, moving with heads down in the wind to cross the rise.

The ponies move in a long file over the brow of the hill and down the shallow combe seeking the shelter of the lower ground. Save for their movement one's eye would hardly see them go, so much are they a part of the moor, and so well does their colouring harmonize and blend with the winter colours of the moor. Dark bay and brown bodies, mealy underparts and blue-black points seem but a reflection of the mahogany red of the sodden bracken, the dark brown of the winter heather, the bleached dun colour of rush and bent and the inky blackness of the newly swaled patches. They move ghost-like, seeming to glide, and in a few moments they are all gone, gone as wild creatures go, swallowed up in the wilderness of the moor.

Wild creatures they surely seem, despite their nominal ownership by the farmers of the hills, living their lives on the open moor, in summer, in winter, in storm and sunshine and snow, handled by man only once a year and dependent only on their own hardiness and courage for survival. Whence came they, these little horses of Exmoor? No one knows, for their remote origin, like that of so much else, is lost in time, but there seems little reason to doubt that the true Exmoor pony is indigenous, and that it indeed represents a remarkable survival into modern times of the original wild horse of prehistoric Britain. Long ago, perhaps, some remnant of the race that once roamed over all Britain and north-west Europe became isolated in these western hills, and here endured in its natural state into historic times, to be subdued by man only in comparatively recent centuries.

Certainly all the points of an Exmoor pony are those one would look for in a wild horse, and in its ways it is closer to wild stock than any other existing breed. The Exmoor colouring is essentially that of a wild creature, such as a deer or an ass. The Exmoor colour can best be described as brown, ranging from red-brown (bay) to dark brown (brown) and sometimes to a flat smoky brown (dun). The colouring of the body is always graduated, the underparts of the belly and the insides of the legs and the back of the buttocks being mealy coloured, while the top of the back is dark, often blackish. The mane, tail and points are a hard black. The most distinctive feature of the race, though, is the mealy muzzle. This, together with the eye cingle or 'toad eye', constitutes the hallmark of the race. No other breed carries this as a distinction, though there are indications that it was once the common badge of all wild horses. No white marks of any sort are permissible on an Exmoor.

In general conformation the true Exmoor is very strongly, though not coarsely, made. The head is strong and straight-nosed, with very deep jaw, broad forehead, small ears set wide apart, bold eye and widely flaring nostrils. The neck, often hollow in young stock, becomes heavily crested in a stallion, and the windpipe is always large and prominent. The body of a mature animal is deep and broad and full of power, though the withers are often rather low and there is a tendency for the rump to droop somewhat towards the tail. In action the tail is carried outwards, pennant-like, not high in Arab fashion. The legs are strong-boned and clean with only a small fetlock tuft, and the hoofs are small, dark and iron hard.

The average height is about 12 hands, though the range is from 11 h.2 to 12 h.2 or a little over for stallions. (This corresponds with the skeletal remains of wild horses from prehistoric deposits.) The coat in summer is fine and glossy, with a polished sheen to it, but in winter it grows thick and bear-like, and the mealy parts are accentuated to an almost flour-like white. The foals are almost always light-coloured at birth, gradually becoming darker as they grow older.

The hardiness, the ability to endure the long winter on the open moor is unparalleled, and is surely an inheritance from the wild.

The earliest historical references to the ponies of Exmoor are from the Domesday Book (A.D. 1086). Here mention is made, in the many entries for the surrounding manors in both Devon and Somerset, of *equae indomitae* and *equae silvestres*. These little wild horses were probably valued even in those early days as foundation stock, and herds were no doubt kept much as they are today.

Throughout the Middle Ages and long after, Exmoor as a royal forest was a huge open grazing ground, and sheep, cattle and horses of all sorts mingled there with the wild ponies. Since, however, the horse stock turned on to the forest from the moorland farms and little villages must itself have been of predominantly Exmoor blood, it is unlikely that this infusion had any effect on the native character of the breed.

By the eighteenth century there are records of a herd of Forest ponies being managed from Simonsbath on behalf of the Forester of Exmoor, and old account-books of the period give some interesting details as to the general management and the annual sale of young stock, etc.

Subsequent to the year 1814, when steps were taken by the

Crown for the disafforestation and sale of Exmoor Forest, all the ponies were driven down off the Forest and sold. Sir Thomas Acland, who had been the last warden, took the best of them and brought them to Winsford Hill. Here they ran for many years as the famous Acland herd, bearing the anchor brand and being managed from Ashway. It is from this Acland herd that many of the best strains and notable herds of today derive. The Acland family had taken great care to maintain the character and purity of the breed, and in 1921 the Exmoor Pony Society was founded to continue this good work and to perpetuate the true and ancient stock.

Today the ponies still run on the commons of Exmoor from Molland to Porlock, even as they once ran on the Forest. It is of course obvious, though, that many of the ponies running on the commons are far from being true Exmoors. During the past century much crossing was resorted to in an attempt to 'improve' local stock according to fashionable standards, and in addition to this all sorts of nondescript horses got turned out on the commons. Extremes of blood from Arab to cart-horse were infused into the general pony stock, with the result that a mongrel race developed, especially on the northern commons. Today the term 'Porlock pony' automatically implies a cross-bred animal.

Of the herds still running on the open moor, those of Withypool Hill are the best and the least mixed. Most of these ponies belong to, or are derived from, the herd of the Miltons of Weatherslade, who, I believe, had some of their stock from the same dispersal sale as did the Aclands.

It is noteworthy that any sort of cross-breeding has the effect of reducing the natural hardiness of the Exmoor. Only ponies of the old stock can survive such a winter of snow as that of 1947 unfed and unhelped on the open moor. In that great winter most of the Exmoor ponies of Withypool Hill came through to the spring unharmed, while the cross-bred ponies suffered terribly and many died. Nevertheless the Exmoor as a foundation stock for breeding first cross riding ponies and small hunters is of the greatest value, transmitting as it does all its good qualities of courage, soundness and sure-footedness.

In strength, courage and endurance the true Exmoor is without equal, as anyone can testify who has ever ridden one. A pony of 12 hands seems very small to mount at first sight, yet such are the substance and temper of the little beast that once one is up he seems to grow in stature and power under the saddle. One feels the driving force of the hind quarters under one like pistons, and the small stride is quite tireless. Neither does such a pony look small even when carrying a full-grown man, so well does he hold himself. In passing it may be noted that in olden times the Exmoor was never referred to as a pony, but as a horse, though its stature has never been greater than today. A little horse—how well does that truly describe this bold, small creature.

As I go home after a day on the moor in the wind and rain and sun I think again of the ponies. How like they are to the drawings of the cave man. As I see them now, so must he have seen them perhaps 20,000 years ago. Now with the lamp lit, I take out my books and papers and turn over the pictures. Here is the red horse from the cave of Altamira with the same small ears and deep, curved jaw and one neat forefoot picked out in black. Here again the wonderful carved head from Mas d'Azil with the ear laid back and the mouth open to neigh—a true pony head. Here are heads with a mealy muzzle clearly indicated, and here horses standing or moving singly or in groups. There is one slab of stone on which two troupes of horses are drawn up in a line, each with its leader. They seem to come alive again, these creatures formed by line and colour, as one's mind goes back to the time when all things were wild. But the fire burns low on the hearth and I am growing sleepy, so the ponies must go back to the hills beyond the ridge of time and I to bed.

§

HALF PAST ten in the morning, and another wild stormy day with a battering sou'west wind and a great sky of clear cold blue and towering, angry clouds all grey-and-white. Half past ten, and I wait in the brown heather near the road and pull my coat tighter against the wind.

The wind is singing in the telegraph wires with the cold sound of ageless space, and it blows the scent of bog and heath strong into one's nostrils and tears at one's clothes like invisible hands, and batters the gorse that has dared to put forth a few first yellow flowers. Sunlight and shadow chase each other in an endless pattern over the brown waste. The moor is alternately exhilarating and sinister as the light changes from shadow to sun and back again to shadow like the passions that play across the human soul. Before me the larks rise from the heather, but they do not sing because of the rough wind. Some distance away by the moorland gate that spans the road a group of horsemen wait in the shelter of the old beech hedge that flares against the sky with still-clinging leaves.

Then suddenly they come, over the skyline and along the old track by the boundary hedge—a dappled wave, light against the dark heather, and two red coats like spots of blood and two tossing bay horses. They come onwards, nearer, and past me, living poetry of form, colour and movement. Horsemen and hounds on the moor—how they seem always to be a living expression of the moor, to be an essential part of it, in some way a fulfilment for which the space and wilderness wait. How one's heart leaps ever at the sight and at the sound of their bodies brushing through the heather.

The meet is small—some twenty horsemen and a few cars and one or two foot-followers. They stand for a little while in a close group, horses and riders, pressed in under the big beech hedge, glad of the shelter. There is talk of a fox on the allotments. Then the huntsman gathers his reins, and the hounds swing out for the moor and the cavalcade of clattering riders follows them into the heather. As they go away over the brow of the moor they seem to ride straight into an arc of blue sky as though to a realm of light and space. Then a sudden shower of hail closes the scene, and when it passes the moor is empty again, save for the wind and the shadows and the running light.

I walk on for a way, and presently sit down amongst the rushes in the shelter of a high bank. Before me, beyond the slope of the moor, is a pattern of fields on a rising hill, and the pale fresh green of them is lovely amongst the brown and gold and shadow-blue of the wasteland. In the midst, like a jewel in a setting of silken colour, a white farmhouse gleams in a sudden shaft of brilliant light.

Suddenly there is a slight rustle and a stoat runs across the grass before me, not a yard from my feet, to the cover of the gorse bank on my right. I have seen stoats before, but never one of quite such a rich colour as this. He is a dark chestnut-red colour, quite mahogany, and as he turns to face me for a second before bolting down an old rabbit-hole, his chest flashes white like a hand's-breadth of snow. He is big for his sort, as big at least as a well-fed, domestic ferret, I should think. I am pleased to see him for this fleeting moment, for his sort is not very common nowadays.

Once there were both polecats and pine martens in these wilder parts of the west, but they have long since become extinct. Rumours do exist to the effect that a few members of the polecat tribe may possibly survive in the wilder fastnesses of the moor, but I think this very unlikely. What is more likely is that a few lost ferrets may have turned feral, and on being seen in what would seem a wild state have been thought to be polecats. After all, the ferret is only a domesticated strain of a variety of polecat, and as animals turning feral always seem to assume the general characteristics of the wild stock very quickly, it would not be unnatural to confuse the identity of one with the other.

Ferrets were, until very recently, the natural complement of every countryman round about, for rabbits were plentiful—indeed excessively so—everywhere on the moor up to the time of the disastrous (for them) outbreak of myxomatosis. I have many memories of rabbiting with dogs, nets and ferrets and also of hours spent trying to recover lost ferrets who for some reason or other refused to come back out of the burrows. Our ferrets were of all colours, but the most popular seem to have been the cream ones, and certainly they were very pretty, if one can use that term of any creature so lethal.

Myxomatosis decimated the rabbit population somewhere around the years from 1953 to 1957 and put an end to the semi-professional rabbiting and the keeping of ferrets, and for a long while there was never a rabbit to be seen about the moor. Now, though, at the time of writing, rabbits are beginning to make a come-back and may soon again become plentiful if their numbers are not checked.

The clouds grow less with the afternoon and their edges turn golden, and they scatter and fly like a shattered armada before the hounding wind of the west.

The cry of a curlew comes up from the rushes, and the murmur of the streams from below. As the sun sinks and the light fades the moor becomes dark and sombre again, almost sinister, yet vast with the infinity of space. One's thoughts turn towards home, and to food and fire and to all small human needs in a cold and measureless void.

The dark forms of the trees and tall hedges against the last glow of the evening sky are like the chords from a mighty symphony as I go home. The clouds heave and sink in huge and awesome shapes upon the night wind, and the loneliness of space is all around, and my footsteps quicken towards the haven of known things and the place that is comfort and safety in the hours of darkness.

§

Our big field stretches out in the late afternoon sun like a pale green cloth—short-bitten turf as smooth as a lawn, hemmed all round with hedges that shine silvery brown in the clear light. The sky above is a pure pale blue with only a few wisps of sailing cloud. A robin trills in the hedge, and somewhere a blackbird pipes. The moss on the beech roots is golden green, and warm under the hand.

Now there is a stir in the field, and the flock of Horn ewes lift their heads and fill the air with their bleating and come running to where the half-bale of sweet-scented hay has been broken and scattered on the grass. They tear it hungrily from the hands that shake it for them, and jostle greedily for as much as they can get, and run from one wisp to another as though afraid that a neighbour has better than they. They clash and butt for a while, and then settle down and spread out in a quiet grazing line once again. Their fleeces are turned to gold by the afternoon sun, and their shadows to violet-blue, and here and there they are touched by shepherds' marks of blue and red like bright heraldic ciphers. Their goat-like horns curve back like antennae. Already they are heavy in lamb, for it is early March, and the first lambing will begin towards the end of the month, and the cycle of life start again on the hill farm.

They are an ancient breed, these Exmoor Horns. They and

their ancestors have existed on the hills of Exmoor for as far back into the past as the memory of man can go, and their small squat bodies and goat-horned heads are a part of the moor and its history. Whence they came no man can say—for the sheep, *Ovis*, is not thought to be indigenous to Britain, but to have come northwards with the Neolithic peoples—but it is certain that they represent one of the oldest strains of sheep in the country. Once, it seems, all sheep were horned, and the older, more primeval form has maintained itself, like certain sorts of horses and cattle, in the remote hill districts of the north and west of our country. These, our horned sheep of Exmoor, would seem to be one remnant of a race known as the Western Horn, a type which once ranged all across the West Country from Wiltshire to Cornwall (the Wiltshire Horn, the Dorset Horn and the now almost extinct Portland are kindred survivals). For many generations they were the only sheep known to the moor, until the coming of the Closewool and the more recent introduction of divers other hill breeds.

The Exmoor Horn of today is doubtless much improved on the original stock. The Exmoor of former times must have been considerably more goat-like, able to exist on the roughest herbage, and to live for most, if not all its life on the open moor. Indeed I have heard it said that originally the rams of the breed used to carry a beard under the chin like male goats, but this characteristic must have long since been bred out, for I have never seen it in a living sheep. One thing, though, has become noticeable in recent years, and that is the effort of breeders to get rid of the over-abundant wool on the face, and so to breed a clean-faced Exmoor. Both sexes of the older type had a tendency to thick wool over most of the face, nearly down to the snout, and such being the thickness of the wool it was not uncommon for a sheep to become quite blind through the matting of the wool over the eyes. I have seen this wool-blindness myself more than once.

The Exmoor today is classed as a mountain breed and its fleece described as being of thick medium-length wool of good quality with an average weight of $5\frac{1}{2}$ to 6 pounds. With regard to the wool, it is a curious but known fact that when the sheep are kept in ground on good grass, as so many are today, the quality of the wool deteriorates. Fine quality can only be maintained by running sheep on the moor, where they feed on the heather and wild grasses.

Though our present Exmoors may lack something of their original hardiness they still retain a good deal of their old independence and obstinacy. Their instinct in hard weather is to scatter, each one to seek for shreds of grass and mosses for itself, digging if necessary through snow and ice with the forefeet in search of such scant sustenance. Young sheep frequently have to be taught to come to hand-feeding, for it is not natural to them as it is to the more domesticated lowland breeds, but they become greedy enough once the idea is accepted.

I turn back towards the farm. Evening. A great glowing sunset with a horizon of pure orange gold under a sky of steel-blue, and black trees like cut silhouettes and a single star bright like an eye in the west. Now a waxing moon shining white on the roofs of the old farm from above a bank of gathering cloud. The sharp bark of a fox somewhere out across the fields and the answering bark of the farm dogs. Night, and I am tired.

Yet I am uneasy and do not sleep. In the darkness the southern horizon is suddenly red all along its rim, a curdled crimson glowing and growing into lurid flame. The swaling fires. The spreading glow reaches into the night, widening and deepening until the clouds above are suffused with the red and the sky itself seems to smoulder and take fire. Somehow, I know not why, I feel disturbed. There is something ominous, foreboding, in that burning hill, that fire in the night. It is like a red omen, though of what I do not know.

The burning fires, the March fires, the fires that blaze the way of spring. Every year in the month of March they burn the moor, setting the flame to leap like a snake amongst the gorse and heather and smoulder under the bent and bracken, charring and blackening all before it. The purpose of the swaling is, of course, to clear off old, coarse, spent growth and to make way for the new, and to discourage the too-heavy growth of scrub. Judiciously used and properly managed it is an excellent and a necessary expedient, but when inexpertly handled it can, I think, become detrimental to the ecology of the moor. Heather is a very slow-growing shrub, and to burn it out year after year is to weaken it before the assault of more resilient and less desirable growths such as dwarf gorse and bracken and coarse grasses. Also continuous annual burning over any given area will ultimately lower the fertility of the soil. Again, to send the fire through the scrub-cover too late in the season—as is so often done—is to destroy the nests of many birds and other small forms of life, and to check all re-growth for that year. Possibly once in ten years might represent the proper cycle for burning a heather moor, though I know this is open to argument.

Certainly great discretion should at all times be used in the burning of the cover on scarps and steep hillsides. A good mat of scrub in such places, though superficially undesirable to the shepherd, is nevertheless nature's best protection against erosion, and should not be too heedlessly destroyed.

§

A MILD grey morning, quiet, still, without any wind. Only the rooks move on the grass, like black goblins, strutting and cawing to one another.

Across the field comes the sound of chopping, and the dull rhythmic thud of an axe on timber. On the far side two men are laying the long beech hedge. As I cross the grass, the hedge rises up dark and grey and I can see them, one man on the bank wielding the axe, and the other now on the ground clatting with a long shovel. Milky-white chips fly from the axe, and the big timbers reel and crash to the ground one after another. The faint, sweet apple scent of the fresh-cut beech wood hangs on the air to mingle with the smell of trampled earth and grass and moss.

It is highly skilled work, this laying of a big beech hedge. All the timber must be cut out clean, right down to the stool, except for a number of young sapling pieces which are left at roughly three or four feet apart to be later cleft and laid in a binding along the top of the bank. The clefts must be sharp and clean so that the rain does not get into the root, and the binding must both edge and criss-cross the top of the bank, so that the sheep cannot get up on to the bank, or should they once do so, they may be prevented from running along the top. (All this must be done while working in precarious positions on the top of a five- or six-foot-high earthen bank and taking care all the time that the heavy timber falls well out over into the fields on both sides.) At the same time the bank must be clatted up, all the hollows and holes under the rootstocks being filled with turfs.

They are wonderful things, these great beech-crested Exmoor banks that hedge all the fields and are such an integral part of the moorland landscape. They are both boundary and wind-break in this storm-swept land, and the shelter they give is amazing. A strong hedge-bank will break the full force of the wind for many times the length of its own height, while close in under the bank one can always find complete shelter even though a sou'west gale is blowing on the other side. In addition to the double purpose of providing both fence and shelter for stock, the beech also serves a third—the provision of firewood. Until recently, beechwood from the big hedges was almost the only fuel, other than peat, used by the hill farms. The length or number of hedges laid each winter would be regulated by the year's requirements of fuel as much as anything else. The old tenancy agreements—or so I believe—stipulated that each hedge be laid once in fifteen years, the tenant keeping the firewood. Many of the big hedges standing today, however, have not been laid for the past twenty or thirty years or more, and the timber in them is as big round as a man's thigh.

Nevertheless, though the beech as a tree is probably native to the region, or at least to the lower parts of it, and has been planted for generations about the farmsteads, it would seem that our beech hedges upon the banks are not themselves of very ancient origin. The fashion of setting the thick cresting of beech along the tops of the field banks seems to have developed about 130 years ago, though from whence the innovation came I do not know. Previous to this the banks would just have been topped with mats of gorse and scrub. Certainly, whatever its origin, the beech is admirably suited to its purpose and is an ideal windbreak, for the wind slips easily off the smooth trunks and does not wrench them, while the roots dig like knotted fingers into the stony earth. It is very rare to see uprooted or splintered beech, and where beech cannot grow upright it will grow horizontally, bowed but unbroken before the wind. Also, young cut-back beech does not shed its leaves, but holds them all the winter until they are pushed off by the spring buds, so making a very thick hedge.

The banks beneath the hedges are immeasurably older. 'As old as time' one might almost say, for the cast-up earthen bank is probably the oldest form of boundary known to man. Such were the first bounds cast up by the first farmers who came to settle on the moor, perhaps a thousand years ago or more. It may be that the banks about the little irregular fields that cluster close to the farms remain just as they were set when the farms were first cut from the moor long ago. On the other hand many are known to have been made in the middle of the last century, when much hitherto open land was enclosed. A good Exmoor bank is about six feet high (though many have sunk lower with the passing of time) and six feet wide or more, at the foundation, sloping slightly inwards to about four feet at the top. The best banks are stone-faced, set with some three feet of dyking on both sides; and again, the making and repairing of this work is an art in itself.

The usual method of building up the dyking of a bank-face is by setting the thin, medium-sized stones upright in level courses, each course tamped in tight with earth, and each stone carefully fitted with hand and hammer. Three, four or even five feet high the dyking may go, and then is capped with two or three feet of sod 'spine'. Newly done and well made, such a facing is as rigid as iron, and impervious to both the horns of bullocks and the scissor-like feet of sheep. Though the upright setting of the stones is the most usual way, a herring-bone form of work is not infrequently to be met with on the western, or Devonian, side of the moor. But whatever the method, what enormous labour must have been expended in the past in the making and dyking of the banks that run everywhere across the country! One has only to watch the present-day repairing of a bank, with all its slow and painstaking work, to marvel at the persistence of a former generation in driving the mile upon mile of new banking out across the moor. Today one shrinks at the very thought of such an undertaking.

Incidentally, out across the wastes of the Forest one frequently comes across a different sort of walling, a plain, dry-stone walling reminiscent of the north country and seemingly outside of the local tradition. These now crumbling walls that run like blue serpents across so many miles of desolate country are the nineteenth-century work of the Knight family, and it is indeed possible that they were built by labour from outside the West Country.

I go on my way. The country is a study in greys and soft blues and browns and pale muffled greens gathered together under an opal grey sky. Presently long shafts of light spear through the cloud, brightening the land for a moment, then withdraw again, leaving the world to its greyness.

Dusk will come early tonight. The days are still short, despite the feeling of spring, and it will be a while yet before the evenings open out. How one looks forward to the lengthening days as one feels the afternoon's light begin to go, and not half the work done that should be.

§

OVER THE hills and down the valleys and into the fields the west wind blows the smell of the moor, the smell of spring. It is the scent of the bogs and the sea, the scent of grass from under the snow, the scent of earth in the sun, the smell of life itself. It is a smell to make an old man young and quicken the blood in the heart. It is a thing to make one shout with the joy of space and the year stretched out before one.

All nature seems to wake; earth and sky call to each other. The green fields slope to the morning sun, green again from under their covering of snow, grassy faces turned to the light of spring. The tall hedges that gird them about reach shining branches to the clear bright sky, full of the twittering of many birds, and over the fields the gulls from the sea wheel and soar like pieces of paper in the wind. Through the silver-gold shafts of the saplings the distant hills lie white-capped in the brittle blue of the west. The frost of dawn is withered away with the light, and the sun is warm on the grass and one's face, and the snow-hills beckon into space, calling one to some fabulous land beyond the gates of time.

How different, how changed, is the scene. Three mornings ago the blizzard struck with driving snow on a bitter wind straight from the eye of the north. I remember the sheep all crowded tight in under the hedges, so hard to find, and the wind a howling gale blowing the snow flat out like smoke from a great white fire, and streaming clouds of white pouring from every gateway, blinding one and biting the face into numbness. I remember the drifts, and every twig and stem, where not torn by the wind, encrusted with snow many times its own girth, and the horizon, where glimpsed through the snow, showing blue-black like a pall pressed down.

Now the sun shines again on the grass, the smell of spring is over the earth—that sweet smell that comes only when the late snow is withering away before the sou'west wind—and the snow lies now only in a few deep drifts by the gateways and on the heights of the moor. As I turn and walk by the hedge other scents catch at me like an undertone—frosted ivy touched by the sun, moss, new timber set across a gap, fir trees somewhere out of sight, wisps of hay left by the sheep, the first opening flowers of the gorse. How potent is the sense of smell, how emotionally powerful. It can move one almost with the force of music. It can excite and delight, it can open doors in the memory closed against all other means, it can create an awareness of things around one like a revelation, or it can lift the mind into realms beyond description. It can also bring apprehension and warning and fear, and the perception of hostile forces. Yet how few people seem to retain a true sense of smell—how few can smell a fir plantation in the sun a mile away or catch the scent of standing corn or tell what animals have been grazing a certain patch of ground, or know whether the grass they tread is old pasture or a new-sown ley.

After the snow the grass is sweet. The sheep spread out on the short pale turf and nibble hungrily at it, but there is never enough to satisfy. The time of growing is not yet, for it is always late in the hills, and one can never be sure of grass until well on in April or even May. All the while the beasts are restless, and one looks anxiously from the dwindling fodder in the barns to the way of the wind and the sun, and hopes desperately for an early spring.

Now is the time when the sheep break out. The hunger for grass is upon them and neither turnips nor hay will satisfy them and their desire. You may put sixty sheep in a field, and find only six when next you go to look at them. Up some corner of bank less staunchly 'gapped' than the rest they will go one after another, pushing their way through and along the hedge at the top until they find a point where they can scramble down and away. Over the fields they will range, over their own and a neighbour's too, and out to the moor beyond. Half one's days seem to be spent finding and fetching them back. All beasts are restless, the cattle as well, and they will go too if they can. Out on the moor the bogs are at their most dangerous. The grass grows first in the middle of the bog, on the eye of the bog, between the water and sun; and hungry beasts are lured by the false green blades, forgetting their natural caution in their desire. Once in the slime of the bog they flounder and struggle in the sucking peat, and many there must be who have not come out again.

The afternoon is as lovely as the morning. The western sun shines still from a cloudless sky, filling the land with a magic light. One feels one is moving in an element of pure light, mystic, wonderful, incomprehensible. But the warm nights of spring are not yet come, and as the shadows lengthen the chill of another frosty evening spreads over the land before the sinking sun.

Across the cold fields comes the wonderful fluting cry of a flock of golden plover, like all the pipes of Pan, from over the hills and far away, lilting down the wind. I turn my face to the west and walk into the glowing golden light. Far off, the long line of the Forest closes the horizon, a sea of silence, a long level wave spilling over towards one. It is all magic and wonder.

Presently dusk folds about the earth. There is no sound now but the murmur of the distant streams and the occasional movement of sheep on the frosty grass. The stars are legion, looking down like eyes of light, and Orion's belt is girded above the trees. I am reluctant to go home and shut out the night. How many people see the stars as I do? Not many in this modern world, I think. We have bartered our heritage for too many other things. Our small lives are hemmed about with fetters of our own making and our souls caught in a web of our own weaving. Who shall set us free? I know not the answer.

April

GOLDEN GORSE like a yellow flame, and sky as blue as a peacock's neck. White sailing clouds, distant fields green as wheat, fox-red beech and the velvet brown of heather. The blazon of April is over the moor again with light and life and colour, and here where I sit for a while are warmth and delight and all the sensuous joy of the spring.

The air is full of the smell of life, the scent of the moor in the sun, and over the bog the curlew calls, that lone cry that is the voice of the moorland spring. Underfoot, under the heather, a little grey lichen has broken into pin-points of scarlet to salute the sun of the stirring year, while along the old boundary bank, just beyond and behind, the whortleberry bushes have decked themselves with their bells of delicate pink, a shower of colour—the first flowers of the moor.

Light, colour, sound, scent, movement and the touch of things under one's hands—for a moment all the senses are drawn together in one perception, no longer separate but one single awareness of life and the delight of life, and of light and space which is in itself a perception beyond the bounds of time. There is no longer time or place, but only the eternal now, and the larks sing for ever in the blue heights.

The clack of a horse's hoofs on the nearby track and a horseman's shoulder over the flaring gorse recall time to the sunlit world. The track runs on to the narrow road, and the road runs down to the river deep under the hill, and that is the way that I must go today. So up and away. The road dives between high enclosure hedges and plunges steeply under the scarp of the hill, all hot in the sun, and the white of blackthorn is like a feathering of cloud along the way. Above, up to the rim of the hill and the sky, the sallow trees lift heads of soft flowery yellow against the blue, like the mimosa of a southern land. Springs of dashing white water pour from clefts in the rocky hill to fall in running rivulets across the roadway. Small ferns uncoil in the crannies and the mosses are emerald cushions. Primroses and delicate wood-sorrels and the blue heath violets gem the steep banks. Everywhere the grass is growing, slim blades rising in every damp and sunny place, over every field and bank, a green herald crying spring.

Under the bridge the river runs full and clear over its bed of stones; but I do not linger now. The road goes on up the high hill beyond, a ribbon between the two banks of rusty bracken, and from the crest all the countryside spreads out like a heaving counterpane. Apple-green fields intermingle with the great tawny gold reaches of moor, all lit with the clear light of the sun and shadowed with the gliding blue of the galleon clouds. Deep combes tumble down to little rough woods and the small glinting streams below. In the midst, on a long shoulder of hill, a white farmstead is set like a note of music calling the eye as an ear is called by a sound.

Horsemen are passing me now, hoofs ringing on the hard road and bridle bits jingling. But here is the inn at last, all alone at the crossroads high on the top of the moor. There's a suggestion of bustle about it today, with coming and going about its doors, and cars pulling up within reach of its low white walls. Riders are coming in from all its four roads, clattering and talking, mounted on horses of every sort—blood-hunters and weight-carriers, cobs and ponies and small handy horses whose mealy noses betoken their Exmoor blood. Some come singly and some in family groups. Some also are coming with the opulence of horseboxes—great juggernauts that jam the narrow ways. The cars are lined along all the roads, or backed into hedges where space allows, and people are everywhere now.

There's an extra stir, and folk make way about the open gate opposite the face of the inn, and here are the hounds again fresh for another day's hunting. Here they come! Big powerful creatures, white and tan and a little black, all bone and muscle, a surge of animal bodies, with the blaze of red coats above them. Into the field they turn and all the horsemen follow, and all the folk on foot as well, all eager to look at the hounds and to discuss the prospects of this, another day's spring stag-hunting. The big hounds drop down in a circle before the huntsman's hoofs, well used to all the attention they receive, and huntsman and master and harbourer confer together in a low-voiced group. A stirrup cup comes out from the inn, and is consumed with appreciation.

Now it's 'Hounds, please', and hounds move out of the field and over the road to kennel in the barn of the inn. A wait of some little while and the tufters are selected and drawn. They emerge, four couples of old steady hounds; the huntsman sounds his horn to the world and they move off down the road and through a gate to the moor. The horsemen fall into a long cavalcade and follow on close behind. On and over the moor they go, along the skyline and over the rim, a hundred riders and more, moving figures against the bright sky like a hundred centaurs loosed from time to trample on the western hills.

Those of us who have no horses turn down the northerly road and across some rough enclosure to where the head of a combe comes in and the hills fall away to a wide wooded view. We wait full of expectation, all senses tensed until the voices of the tufters are heard somewhere in the woods below. There are deer afoot somewhere down there now, but more than that we

34

cannot tell. The cry of the hounds comes intermittently, now up, now down the valley, and the occasional sound of the huntsman's horn and voice encouraging them, but there is nothing to be seen in the thickness of trees. Presently the sounds get fainter and farther away—the stag, if indeed they have found him, has gone down the valley, down the long wood that runs westward into Devon. Someone with powerful field-glasses declares he can see the pack going out somewhere along the top of the far wood, hastening to the lay-on. So the stag is away, and heading on into the maze of wooded valleys that lie about the feet of the hills.

Reluctantly I turn and retrace my steps back over the windy hills and the tawny-gold moor. The way home seems long. Half way I slip down to a stream to drink. How lovely are these April streams, the very spirit of living water, crystal clear, white and foaming over rock and ledges; then gliding in pools of pure amber, golden, translucent, rippling like running silk, each pool holding the sunlight in its depths as clear as light. Every stone at the bed of each is mirror-clear, bathed in shimmering gold. One stands half mesmerized gazing into the depths of these pools of silken gold. They hold a magic all their own. I do not know their secret, but their draught of water is sweet and cool in the sun, and quenches one's thirst.

Back to the road again and on to the hill with my face towards home, and then down the west wind afar off, yet drawing nearer, I hear the cry of the hounds. The stag must have doubled back and be heading this way. Yes, the hounds are coming nearer and the deer cannot be far away. There he is. For a moment I see him, poised for a second on the top of a bank as he leaps up and over. A lean brown beast, brow, trey and uprights on top, a spring stag, a 'light-galloping toad'. I see a flash of his lemon-white rump, and then he is gone. A space, and then the hounds come, running hard to keep on terms with their deer, strung out in a long file like a trailing chain, giving little tongue now because the pace is so fast and uphill. Hoofs drum on the sod behind them, and here come the huntsman and the hard-riding vanguard of the field, galloping as hard as their horses can go to keep pace with the running pack and hold them in sound and view. Now the rest of the horsemen are coming from all directions over the moor, through the fields, down the road and down the steep sides of the combes and up again, and on to the river that runs by the bridge. The stag has crossed the river, and risen the farther moor, and the pack are struggling up the heathery slopes, so far on that the eye can scarcely hold them. How says the song? 'The quarry's a dancing midge, the pack's a string of struggling ants!' True enough out on the rolling moor with a spring stag well in front. How far will he go today? Fifteen miles, twenty miles, perhaps, or more. Not many who rode to the meet will see the end of the run, only those well mounted on the best of horses, whose resolution is bold and who know the country well from every ford to every gate.

The old staghounds of the eighteenth century who kennelled at Highercombe and Castle Hill could never have hunted a flying spring stag. The old pack, the North Devon Staghounds, the pride of the Acland family, were massive brutes, huge even against the modern staghound, and very slow, depending on nose and perseverance to bring a stag to bay. I once saw an old painting of them, and they seemed like something between a bloodhound and a mastiff. The modern staghound, of foxhound origin, is fast enough to keep on terms with the deer by his speed; though even so he is hard put to it to take a spring stag.

§

HILL MIST. A world of absolute blankness. Here on the edge of the moor the heather is black at my feet, then, reaching out, is swallowed in a white nothingness that is blind, empty and soundless. Nothing stirs. The fog is at once a muffling blanket and an utter lifeless emptiness. It is without form or meaning or dimension, like the void before creation.

Back in the fields the hedges loom up out of the blankness like grey walls, strangely huge and towering. Sheep appear from the void like ghosts. An old cart set as a scratching-post materializes as a strange abstract thing in the middle of a meadow. Everything is strange and unreal. All things appear larger than they really are, a sheep as a bullock and a hayrick as a mountain, and all distance is distorted. Stationary objects seem to advance towards one. One's senses become bewildered, and even in one's own fields the familiar seems unreal and insubstantial.

The breath of the mist is wet on my face, and all the hedges drip with the wetness. The sheep begin to stir at sound of the human footstep, bleating one to another out of the fog, reminded of the breakfast they have not yet had. This hill mist, so much a part of our moorland weather, at all seasons, is the shepherd's nightmare. To 'see sheep', to search for a missing sheep in this opaque whiteness, is all but impossible, like trying to see with eyes that are blind.

At least there is certainty of whereabouts here in the fields. Out beyond the security of the hedges the moor is an engulfing ocean. A wise man does not leave a road or track in this weather, for not only does the mist blot out all landmarks, but unlike the darkness of night it deadens all sense of direction. I have heard many tales of men being lost or fogbound on the moor—even men bred to the moor—of their seeming to blunder round in circles until stumbling by lucky chance on some track or landmark. I never heard of anyone dying of exhaustion or exposure through being lost in an Exmoor fog, but such a thing is not impossible, for once a real hill mist claps in it may not lift for two or three days. Often the mist comes quickly, what has been just a light misty drizzle thickening without warning to an opaque whiteness that closes about one like the circle of a tent. Or perhaps it may suddenly advance over clear ground like a white wall, moving swiftly down to engulf one. If one should be caught thus in the fog, on trackless ground, one at once moves downhill, for hill mist is always thickest on high ground, and anyway, by following a stream down its course, one is always brought ultimately to fields and farms. If one is on level ground, then one feels for the wind—if there is any—and taking its direction in conjunction with a rough knowledge of one's whereabouts, one sets a course towards some known objective. Only once have I been lost in fog on the moor, and on that occasion found my way safely back to a track by walking into the wind, but the experience was not a pleasant one.

Here is the farm again, its walls rising up gaunt and dark amongst the wet trees. All about the place is a welter of mud, squelching, splashing, dragging at one's boots, making a morass of the gateways and a slippery hazard of the yards. The wetness of the fog, condensing on roof and tree, drips miserably from every eave and branch. Everything is desolation and discomfort. All things are clammy to the touch. Only the thought of the kitchen fire within is cheering.

On such a day all work goes slowly; neither man nor beast shows much vigour. The only briskness is the throbbing of an engine and the sharp whine and screech of the buzz-saw from the shed where beech logs are being sawn for the fire. The day drags, yet dusk comes early. All things dissolve in a grey emptiness that deepens into night. Yet a night of fog is seldom a black one. There is a certain luminosity in the hill mist that softens the darkness. The opaqueness, though, will baffle any lantern—the stronger the light the more intense the whitish wall that presses round it.

It is on the dusk of such a day as this that one may see the 'spectre of the Brocken'. Not many see it, yet some do. I once stood in a field at nightfall with a light behind me, and saw a great shadowy figure of myself rise upstanding before me. It was a strange experience.

Home is the best place tonight, though, and I am glad to be at home, safe in the circle of lamplight and known things.

§

ACROSS THE field by the farm comes the plaintive calling of new-born lambs, and the anxious answering bleats of ewes. April is lambing time in the hill country, the busiest time of all the year for the hill farmer. Now for at least three weeks one must be with the ewes day and night, sitting up at nights or at least rising every three hours to make the seemingly endless rounds of the lambing field. Now one must be ceaselessly occupied with difficult births, post-natal sickness, orphan lambs that have lost their mothers, lambs that won't suck, ewes that have no milk, lambs that get lost and always the ever-present danger of attack by foxes, crows and ravens.

One prays for good weather at lambing time—days and nights that are fine and dry and not too cold. Wet weather is a misery, especially as is so often the case at this time of the year, when it 'sets in misty-wet' and the soft rain falls ceaselessly day after day until all the ground is a liquid mess with no dry spot anywhere, and the wet hill mist closes in so that one cannot see the ewes from more than a few yards away. Worst of all is hard frost and snow on a north wind. Then the lambs may freeze to the ground as they fall, or be smothered in snow, and one's hands become numb and fumbling as one goes about the work.

The Exmoor Horns are strange little sheep, and in many ways the strangest of all at lambing time. In the lambing field they will always contrive to go up to the farthest corner of all to lamb; and if it is a big field and bad weather one does not exactly bless them for this trait. They may or may not be good mothers with a single lamb, but almost all of them seem to have rooted objection to doubles, or twins, and when nature so provides one must always be on the watch with them lest they abandon one of the infants at the first opportunity. Sometimes a ewe with a double will take so rooted a dislike to one of the pair that she will turn on it and batter it with her horns, until it has to be taken right away for the sake of its life. When they do look with favour on their offspring they can indeed be good parents, attentive and quick to use their horns on any intruding dog, and they are most talkative to their young, speaking to their new-born lambs with a continuous conversation of muttering sheep-noises.

Exmoors, though very hardy and independent in most ways, have one characteristic, or at least a characteristic that is apparent in the present-day breed, that makes for difficulty and unpopularity at lambing time. This peculiarity is the square top to the head formed by the strong horn development. Young lambs, especially tup-lambs, tend to have big wide-topped heads with the horn bud often developed before birth, and a ewe down to lamb may have difficulty in expelling the head. For that reason the Closewool and other polled breeds tend to be considerably more popular amongst the less conservative breeders, though of course this is not the main reason for the introduction of the latter. The Devon Closewool was developed and bred up from a cross between the Exmoor Horn and the old Devon Longwool in an effort to evolve a sheep having more substance and somewhat heavier wool than the former, though retaining something of the upland hardiness, but of a sort that would be better suited to the improved grassland of progressive farming times. The Closewool inherited the polled head of the Longwool, and so far as I know has never shown any tendency to throw back to a horned state.

Another polled in-ground breed that has become increasingly popular in recent years is the Dorset Down. These are fine-looking sheep, with their lilac-grey ears, black noses and black legs—they are commonly called 'blackfaces' though must not be confused with the Scotch Blackface—and surprisingly enough do very well on quite high ground. Dorset rams are increasingly used for crossing with both Exmoor and Closewool ewes, in order to obtain early fat lambs for the market, and in the former mating it is noticeable that the polled factor is always passed on to the offspring. Border Leicester rams are also used for crossing with Exmoor ewes for early lamb production.

Our ewes are always lambed in the open field on 'clean ground', and then the lambs are 'brought down' with their dams to be housed for the first few nights of their lives in whatever buildings are available. Such a business it is too—bringing them down. Exmoor ewes seem extremely silly in this matter, for time and again a ewe will desert the new-born lamb carefully carried before her and rush back to the spot where she first dropped it. Then there is nothing to do but put the little creature down and hope that it will give the plaintive bleat that will bring her running to it. Incidentally it is strange to note that a ewe seems to recognize her lamb from births onwards, not by sight or even primarily by smell, but by *sound*, by the voice of its bleating. And what a business it is finding accommodation for all the small families. Every possible building that is available is turned out and cleaned and strawed for the daily and nightly reception. Of course every farm has a proper lambing shed with half a dozen neat pens, but of what use is this when the ewes are coming down ten a day?

The necessity for housing is due mainly to the prevalence and rapacity of the foxes. Hill foxes are strong and bold and daring beyond the understanding of the lowland country Reynard. They prowl like wolves in the night—and even in broad daylight— and sometimes a hill farmer will even ring his lambing field with storm lanterns in the hope that by this he may deter the marauders, as foxes are said not to approach a light in the darkness. A new-born lamb is an easy prey and a cheap meal for a hungry fox, and a fox may even take the head of a lamb at the first moment of birth if the ewes are unattended and away from human habitation. Once the lambs are a few days old and 'have their legs' they are usually safe enough and can lie out in peace with their dams.

Another menace is the crow, and by 'crow' a west-countryman means any black member of the corvine tribe, whether rook, crow or raven. All or any of these will attack a ewe in difficulties and like the foxes will take the head of a lamb at birth. Nature is raw and cruel here, and there is little mercy for anything weak or helpless.

Once the lambs are over their first infancy and skipping in the green grass fields, how pretty they are! Exmoor lambs are the child's picture-book lamb come to life—so very white, all soft fluffy wool, with chubby inquiring faces and budding horns like the horns of elves or an infant Pan. The Closewools are similar but without the horn-buds. The Dorsets too are pretty, though in a different way, with short, tight wool that is lilac-grey rather than white, and black heads and black legs that look as though they had stockings on them.

Sometimes one may see a black Exmoor lamb, coal-black, with perhaps just a tip of white to its tail. They are uncommon but do occasionally crop up in some flocks for no apparent reason. Adult black Exmoors are even more uncommon, since being unpopular they are usually got rid of as quickly as possible at an early stage of life, but I did see one black ewe a little while ago. She had a coal-black head out of which her horns protruded at a satanic angle, while her eyes seemed to glitter in her dark face, and the ruffs of dark wool gave the impression of an encircling beard, so that altogether she presented a rather diabolical appearance in the fading evening light in which I saw her. The rest of her fleece was a dark smoky-grey.

Now night-time comes again and all too soon. We bring down the ewes to the small fields by the house and gather in all the day's infants and their mothers to the penned-up sheds, and prepare the lanterns for the night.

As once shepherds 'watched their flocks by night' so we do now. Our ewes are for this space of time at least the prevailing influence in our lives. For this while, and in this pastoral country, the psalms live again, vivid in a world where men are shepherds and all one's life and livelihood depend upon the flocks and herds, and the fate of all upon the seasons and the weather. Again one stands beside the sheep under the stars between the mystery of birth and death, and is conscious of the beasts and of oneself and of the greater mystery for which there is no word.

§

ANOTHER April day—all blue sky and sailing clouds, and sun that is warm enough for May. The road that winds along under the moor is full of the joy of the morning. Tufts of primroses make splashes of butter-yellow in the grassy banks, and little cascades of violets fall down to meet them. Rowan and thorn open fluttering fresh green leaves along the lines of still-brown beech, and green are the fields beyond the hedges. The water of yesterday's rain trickles bright in all the gutters and gulleys, while high overhead a buzzard soars on motionless wings in the dazzling eye of the sun.

Up and away from the bright green fields the moor is tawny and brown, lit by the golden blaze of the gorse on the sunnier slopes. The bleached sedge under my feet squelches in its matrix of sphagnum moss, and the heather is lifeless still, but over the rim of the ridge the wind-stunted larches of the little battered plantation have answered the call of spring and put forth a covering of delicate green. A blackcock bursts forth explosively from a patch of scrub and flies off in noisy annoyance. Blackcock are still to be found on most parts of the heathery moor, but these handsome birds are not plentiful, for the crows take a heavy toll of their eggs. A little farther on I almost step on a fox asleep under a close mat of gorse, and he too goes off in swift indignation.

Down again from the moor the deep woods stand above the river and drowse in the sun, and the sunlight shines through the lattice of bare branches on to the polished trunks that rise as pillars from the earth. At their feet, white windflowers look up like stars from the clutter of last year's leaves, and amongst them the tinier wood-sorrels nod. The river sings to the midday sun, and I go my way over the bridge of stone and up to the hill again.

By late afternoon my walk has brought me round to the long steep scarp that towers above the middle Exe. Rocks like teeth thrust through the shaggy lips of the winter bracken, and thorn and rowan cling to the precipitous slopes that drop to the noisy river far below. On the farther side the gorse is a yellow fire on the slopes above the river. It is a wild spot, little frequented except by sheep and foxes. Wild enough to be the last stronghold of the wild cat in southern England—for, if indeed what I believe is true, a last remnant of *Felis silvestris* survived here on Room Hill until the first years of this century and to within living memory.

It was only recently that I heard the full story of the cats of Room Hill. I had previously heard odd references made from time to time to the wild cats that used to live on Room Hill but I had paid little attention to them, as 'wild cats', that is to say, cats of domestic origin that had turned feral and taken to living and breeding in a wild state, used to be of very common occurrence in the West Country. Then one day a farmer friend who has lived all his life on his farm just under the hill began to talk about 'the cats' and to say things about them that were most unusual and extremely interesting. I asked for as much information as he could give, and this is what he told me.

Long ago, and up to the beginning of this century, Room Hill was the home of a race of fierce wild cats. In the days when he was a boy, fifty or more years ago, there was still a family of them living in the rocks on the scarp of Long Combe, or Curr Cleeve, on the north edge above the Exe. For the most part they kept to the isolation of the hill, but in a hard winter they would come prowling up over the hill and down towards the farm in search of any sort of small prey. Their yowl in the night was a terrifying sound. They were noted above all for their ferocity, and if by day one of them was seen lurking anywhere near the farm the children were ordered to gather up all the domestic cats and other small pets and go indoors with them while father went out with a gun. These wild cats would kill and carry off any domestic cat, and the yard cats were terrified of them.

43

Likewise no dog would dare to attack such a cat, but just ran away at the first encounter.

Now and again he—my friend—would catch a glimpse of one of them, and he vividly remembered how once he came out of the yard just as one came slinking down the lane in broad daylight. So great an impression did the sight of the thing make on him that he never forgot its startling appearance. It was, he said, about the size of a dog-fox. In colour it was grey or tawny-grey, marked all over with dark stripes. Its head was huge in comparison with that of an ordinary cat, and its teeth protruded below the lip like fangs. Its tail was thick and blunt and hung in a distinctive curve behind it. The creature seemed tall on the leg, especially in the hind quarters, and it moved with a sort of slouching gait. To a small boy (as he was then) there was something very frightening in the whole appearance of this remarkable cat.

The last of these cats of Room Hill seem to have become extinct in the years immediately preceding the First World War, exterminated no doubt by trap and gun, for subsequent to this no more were ever seen about the district. I asked if any skins had ever been kept from shot animals, but he said no, he had never heard of any.

So the cats of Room Hill remain a mystery and a tale, though I myself have no doubt as to their origin and species, and regret that they could not have survived a little longer.

§

THE WIND blows fresh from the west on a morning joyful after days of rain, and the moor rolls on before the eye in a great expanse of brown and gold and indigo black under a sky that is massed with huge clouds that mount up in great hammer-heads from the rim of the world. Patches of sunlight break from the cracks of sky to run all the while in moving radiance across the land. The only sound is the wind licking at the rushes and the brown heather.

The going is rough and wet, but the wind and sun are good, and one walks onwards and upwards into space. A small flock of Blackface sheep appear over the skyline, and move down the side of a little combe. Something somewhere has disturbed them. They bunch nervously, their horned mottled faces raised, their lank fleeces light against the shadow. The sudden animal movement awakens something deep within one, like a kindling flame.

Now the hills rise to a heavy skyline, shouldering up from goyals and narrow combes where the streams rip deep beds out of the rock and small rowans dig their roots in the shale. On the rim high on the horizon the ancient barrow lifts dark against the sky, lonely in space, like a hieroglyph speaking from the past to the immeasurable arc above. I come up to it slowly, for the crest is a steady rise and the heather thick, and the wind head-on and strong. It draws nearer, and at last I can scramble up on to it, and turn about and admire the wide and rolling view, and then sit down in the shelter of its earthen rim, tucked under the wind.

It crowns the hilltop with mystery, this desolate mound of earth holding only a forgotten meaning. Low and round, hollow-centred, matted with heather and sunk in rushes, its sides worn and trampled by the hoofs of centuries, it holds silence under the sky. It looks from the hill to other hills across all the expanse of moor and the distant patchwork of little fields, and there more barrows lift their heads on far-off skylines. What men, what hands of long ago, raised these strange round tumps to crest the lonely windswept heights? There are so many of them on the sea-girt hills of Exmoor. There is not a hill or ridge that has not its barrow, and many have more than one. There are eleven in the Chapman Barrows group, which is probably the greatest number together anywhere on the moor. There are seven, I believe, on the Five Barrows ridge (so called because only five are visible on the skyline from any one point) and three—the Wambarrows—on Winsford Hill. There are two or three in many other places, and the single ones are legion. Altogether there must be some hundreds of them. They are all circular in shape, and most of them would seem to be hollow in the middle like saucers. Beyond the acceptance that they are memorials of the Bronze Age, and that they must date from somewhere between 1000 and 1800 B.C., little or nothing is known of them.

There is something strangely compelling about these lonely

45

round tumuli. Burial mounds they are known to be, and under them must rest the great ones of a forgotten race. Chieftains and warriors, priests and bards, perhaps, brought here to lie under the earth and stone, under the sky, under the whistling wind, on the hilltops bare to the sailing clouds. Who they were and why they came we do not know. They can only speak in dreams.

Perhaps they came, these people of the barrows, bearing their illustrious dead, because the stormswept hills, lifted to the western sunset, had some sacred significance for them. To all peoples of the ancient world the hills and mountains were sacramental and they went up into the high places to worship their gods. 'I will lift up mine eyes unto the hills, from whence cometh my help. . . .' Whether or not they themselves dwelt on the high moor no one can say. Unless the climate was drier than it is today it would be a very grim and inhospitable land in winter to a people who were probably largely nomadic, and dwellers in tents or booths (a few supposed hut-circles, which may or may not be of the same date as the barrows, exist on the moor; but these are very few against the vast number of tumuli). Probably they lived for the most part on the lower land about the moor, on the edge of the forest, and came up to the high moor only in summer, for hunting and pasturing of herds, and for the performance of sacred rites.

Perhaps they were the first of all men to try to tame the little wild horses, for probably they were a people of substantially the same stock as the Homeric heroes, the Achean and Trojan 'tamers of horses'. The Bronze Age people are known to have been the first folk to possess and use horses in early Britain, for bridle-bits and other pieces of horse furniture have been found in various places in the country. Superstition associates ghostly horses with at least two of the Exmoor earthworks—the 'noise of the trampling of horses' at Broken Barrow, and the supposed appearance of horses and chariots at Mounsey Castle.

As I rise and bestir myself to come down from Barrow, I see the figures of three men on horseback coming up over the rise towards me. Tossing manes, and brown tweed caps and coats— three hunting farmers out for the day—and, yes, they have hounds with them, four or five couple. Now I know what has disturbed the sheep this morning. Hounds must have been hunting somewhere behind the hills and the pack has divided, and now these honorary whippers-in have collected some hounds and are taking them on to rejoin the huntsmen. They trot briskly past me, calling a greeting as they go, and brush on through the rush bed. Then, suddenly, just as they turn down the slope, hounds hit off the drag of a fox in the rushes— a unified cry, and they're off, heedless of any authority. A burst of laughter from the erstwhile whips, and then they too are off, galloping away on a hunt of their own, disappearing swiftly in the wake of the running hounds. I wonder if they will come up with their fox and if they will kill him then.

Late in the day as I come home in the dimming light I again pass by a barrow low and sunk in the heather, a black hump against a yellow sky, silent in a waste of moor. It is eerie now, with night closing round and the coldness of dusk chilling one's heart. For a moment I feel half afraid as I pass the barrow, though of what I do not know. I catch myself jumping unreasonably as a solitary, wind-battered gorse bush comes suddenly into my line of vision. There is a loneliness yet a sense of being not alone that reaches at one here. Thoughts of home suddenly seem good, and I quicken my pace before the coming darkness.

May

BLUE SKY, pale and hazy with heat, blue hills distant like the frontiers of a fabled land, the heavy flooding scent of golden gorse, green leaves lifted to the light, the hot brilliance of the mounting sun, the lazy call of a bird—the idyll of a May day.

The moor stretches out in all the warmth and light, answering at last the voice of summer with the stirring of shoots and buds and many little flowers. Now the whortleberry beds make splashes of glowing orange amongst the darker heath as the sun catches at all the young red-gold shoots and small new leaves. Here and there amongst the heather bright yellow tufts of the little whin blossom like rosettes of tiny gorse, each minute bush spurred under its flowers with spines in imitation of its greater relatives. Even the heather itself takes on a livelier colour as the reddish-green shoots break from the old brown growth. Across the patches of shorter herbage, swaled perhaps two years ago, a carpet of tiny flowers spreads like a tapestry of bright threads, all interwoven with the short grass and heather shoots. Milkworts, blue and white, yellow tormentil, the rose-cerise of lesser redrattle, violet heath speedwell, threads of white woodruff, all no more than an inch and a half high, scattering the ground with mingled colour. The milkworts, one may note, are of three distinct colours: creamy-white, pale powder-blue, and a rich brilliant sapphire. For added variety a few odd threads of pink or crimson are to be found occasionally.

In the depths of the bog, where the snipe rise with twisting flight from amongst the rushes, the bogbean raises its stately flower above the pools: a spike of small white stars like upturned lily-heads, each petal downy like cut velvet, with a flush of pink beneath as though a pulse beat in its flesh. The gorse is a blaze of yellow fire on the shoulders of all combes and the scent of it presses on one as one lies sprawled in the grass below. On the steep slopes the new stiff patriarchal staffs of the young bracken thrust up from under the brown winter mat, and the hedges green with leaf tumble down to meet the springing brake.

Everywhere the beech has burst into such a glory of living green as bewilders all the senses. Translucent, soft as silk, delicate as fluttering wings, holding the light in showers of pure green-gold—the beech leaves break over the harsh moorland landscape like a benediction, like a voice proclaiming life. Over hill and combe, all round the fields and about the grey-roofed farms the green tide flows and tosses, life from the brown shucked bud, life from the dead wood, life reaching out to the mounting summer sun. How lovely is the beech! No foliage is there more delicate in spring, no leaves so fiery in autumn, nor yet any tree stouter to face the winter gales. It is worthy of a place in heaven if such there be.

Over the leafy hedges, in from the moor, the fields lie thick with grass under the lazy sky, white with the froth of daisies like a reflection of summer clouds on the earth, and starred with the gold of buttercups. Across the grass the sheep spread in a grazing garland, the white lambs skipping about the ewes or asleep under the sunny banks. A cuckoo calls all the time from the hedge, and many birds sing all around. Oh, pastoral May! oh, bright May days! all sunshine and joy, all sky and little white clouds and living grass, like the first youth of all the world.

The cattle too are in the fields, released at last from the yards and shippons, their great red bodies moving lazily in a bovine elysium of green. Soon they will go out to the moor, and so too will many of the sheep. May marks the change in the herdsman's year, the turning from winter to summer. Our ancestors long, long ago divided the year into two equal halves of summer and winter, with two festival days to mark the changing. Beltain and Samhain they called these pagan feast-days, the one at the beginning of May and the other at the end of October. These are the pastoralist's seasons, and their turning-points are far more vital to him than the solstices of Yule and Midsummer. Today we have forgotten the ancient festivals and the unrecorded gods, but still we think of May as the month when the cattle and sheep go out to the hill, and the end of October as the time when they start to come in again.

Sunshine and sky and green growing things, light and space and the promise of life—oh, joyous May, the mirror of heaven, the door of the blessed land! To lie in the golden warmth under yellow gorse and fill one's soul with the flooding scent, to eat and to drink, to watch the sun arching into the west in the heat of the afternoon, to hear the spring birds call. To touch the smooth stones warmed by the sun and the small flowers flickering under one's fingers, and feel the soft grass smooth against one's arms. To live for a moment that is all eternity.

Now I walk home in the evening hours, with all the sky an ocean of endless radiant light about the transcendent glory of the setting sun, and see the hills dissolve in molten space, and all the leaves, each one a green translucent thing, a green light against the light. The sun sinks down and is gone. The horizon grows dark with a line of wind-twisted beech marching along its rim, far off and distant like a drawing. The sense of space and distance is enormous, infinite. It is like looking at a country far off in space and time. It is as though a hand beckoned or a voice called from that long mysterious horizon. The dark skyline against the light seems to draw one's soul. One feels an urge to cry out. Suddenly all things seem possible, for one feels a power that is more than mortal all around. It is an awareness that is something beyond all human understanding.

The hollow drumming of a snipe comes strange and vibrant in the silence. I turn through the first field gate in the twilight, and the last sound of the night is the croaking of the frogs like inane laughter in the labyrinth of the bog below.

§

THE WOODS tumble down the steep slopes in all the colours of May, in all the greens and golds of spring and the first bright flush of summer. Here in the mingled wood the many trees toss their heads together in a delicate glory of first foliage, and the sun shines on the translucent green-gold of beech, the glowing bronze of the oak, the silver-green of the sallow, on all other shades of green and growing things, and the sharper green of the thorns that hem the wood about, till every leaf sings praise to the light. Now is the winter fled away, and the call of the wood pigeons is like the song of the turtle-dove long ago in a far-off land.

Under the trees, deep down the slope, the bluebells make a carpet that is like a reflection of the sky. Once again I walk in the bluebell-wood and my feet rustle the stiff leaves and my hands pick the smooth sap-filled stalks. The strange sultry scent from the heads reaches to me, and unlocks a door on half-forgotten childhood. Bluebells in the wood. I will remember them when I have forgotten all my country's laws and all the words that were ever written.

Above the wood the grass is green and growing, and here where the thickets meet the field one scuffs now in the fern, hopeful of finding a fallen antler. Yet very seldom is it that one does find one, seek as one will. What is the mystery of the shed antlers? What does in fact happen to them? I don't know Every year, every spring, late in April or early in May, all stags shuck their antlers like a child shedding its first teeth, and

51

then retire to the depths of wood and brake to await the growth of new ones. As the numbers of stags and male deer on Exmoor must run into many hundreds, and as antler is a fairly indestructible substance, one would expect that during the course of years many thousands of antlers would accumulate about those places that are most frequented by the deer. Yet, as I have said, only a very few are found. It is sometimes said that the fallen antlers are eaten by the hinds. It may indeed be quite possible that various creatures, including the deer themselves, do gnaw them as a source of calcium. But, again, I don't know.

Those cast antlers which it is a passer's good fortune to pick up are highly prized, or used to be; for it is said to be good luck to find one (I have one—a small antler of a young deer, probably a three-year old, and the mark of shedding is plainly visible below the burr). If anyone is lucky enough to find or obtain two that make a pair, then they are usually set up together on a carved oak shield to hang on the wall. In this latter case they can always be distinguished from a real head by the absence of a skull-top.

Now I turn down the path that leads from the top of the wood to the meadows on the shoulder of the hill that curves round to face the sun. Bracken and then earth gives way to slippery rock as the path plunges down under the trees, and one must go carefully and hold on to branches here and there, else a fall is scarcely avoided, for the stone of the hills is polished smooth with the weather of years and wet with the morning breath of the woods. At last the gate to the open grass is reached and one's feet are safe on the bright green turf again. I follow the slope of the fields down to a rutted track leading to a knot of roofs that beckon from over the hedges, and through one gate and another, and am in a neighbour's yard once again.

Here is yet another old hill farm, a slate-roofed house looking into a stony yard, an L-shape of low-eaved shippons to flank it, and a view of the moor beyond the walls. Chickens and turkeys strut haphazard about the sun-filled square and somewhere a dog barks from the depths of a building. A border of flowers makes a bright edge before the house, protected by a small fence upon a wall. A gate at the side of the yard is raised to the level of importance by the entry thereby of a new road, coming across the fields and deserting the ancient and very narrow lane below. The chief feature, though, of the old farm is the long pillared cart-linhay that still stands with dignity amongst the nettles.

The old cart-linhay stands outside the main yard, just across what was once the laneway entrance to the farm and now is nothing in particular. Four fine round drum pillars rise from the stinging-nettles to support the timbers of the old slate roof that is full of gaps and holes, and behind them, against the plain back wall, are the bits and pieces of the various carts that once rattled cheerfully in and out between them. A tangle of climbing ivy claws its way up the far end to crest one gable with green, and now the swallows have nested in the rafters and fly unhindered through the spaces. Two odd wheels lean stupidly against a pillar with the nettles lacing the spokes and rims. The warm sun shines quietly about the pillars and on all the bits of wood and stone and growing things.

The pillars are beautifully made. The stones of various sorts and sizes are set in a perfect round so that each pillar is a cylinder of some two feet six inches in diameter, broadening slightly at the base, and about seven feet high. Their width apart is just enough to allow the passage of a cart between them, but not, alas, that of a modern implement! Hence the abandonment of the linhay as a useful shelter building.

These fine round-pillared cart-linhays were once a handsome feature of many of the older Exmoor farms, and a number of them still remain. Eastwards and southwards from Simonsbath you will find a good many, some in good repair, some tumbling down and some partly reconstructed to other uses, and hardly recognizable for what they were. Happiest are those whose pillars are set wide enough to accommodate a modern tractor and its tackle, for these can and do still fulfil their original purpose. Four pillars in a row on one open side seems to have been the general rule, though some have only two between walled ends.

The construction of round pillars seems to have been a local practice in the Exmoor districts, for they are themselves a feature of Exmoor building. In various places one can still come across field gateways with fine round stone gate-pillars set on either side, and also one may occasionally see such pillars used as an ornamental feature to a comparatively modern building. The finest remaining field gate-piers that I know are those that occur on the Wellshead–Alderman's Barrow road, but here also, alas! one of each pair is in the process of being pulled down in order to widen the gateway for the passage of modern implements. One wonders how and why the fashion for round pillars originated in this severe region not at all given to architectural embellishment. It may have been that the rounded form arose as a solution to the difficulty of making a satisfactory quoin to the angle of a pillar with the awkward rag or rubble stone to hand. In a few places the ragwork angle of barn or shippon may be rounded. Certainly the rounding of gate or linhay pillars has the added advantage of its being easier to back or turn a cart about such round piers than around angular ones. Just how such pillars were built I do not know—they are always beautifully made and perfectly cylindrical—but someone did tell me that the old builders began by driving a stake into the ground and then working round it with the masonry. However, as I have never investigated the middle of one, I do not know whether this is true or not.

Another noteworthy and often quite imposing local feature arising from the circular pillar form is the round farmhouse chimney. These round chimneys are to be found mostly on the eastward side of the moor, and may be either thick and squat or quite tall and slender. I do not know how old they are, or from what period they first date, but they are very attractive and distinctive.

How sad it is that all our small, local, intimate features seem fated to disappear from the land. Under the relentless hand of modern uniformity all the little pleasing things of local being, those things that are the growth and character of an individual soil, are slowly being crushed into extinction. The texture of material, the shape of a gable, the form of a chimney, the pattern of a gate—how these quiet and unobtrusive features, peculiar to themselves and to the soil that gave them being, evoke the spirit of that soil and tell us more than any words.

§

ACROSS THE lane on this sunny morning late in spring the big blue tractor drones like a bumble-bee in the old stubble field, busy with the last of the spring ploughing and making the most of the fine bright weather. Behind the plough come the gulls, crying with the voice of the sea, wheeling and pitching over the new-turned furrows. How white they are in the sun! They are the big herring-gulls—almost the only sort that we see here—the wide-winged birds of the Atlantic coast. Unfortunately they are looked on with suspicion by the local farmers, who say they kill lambs. This I do not believe, though, of course, being carrion eaters they no doubt would maul any dead carcass left lying about.

While the heavy machinery goes ponderously about the main business of the day we take the old horse from the stable to do a lesser task, that of collecting stakes and wire from the eaten-out turnip ground. The cart harness having been loaded on to the horse, we splash across the yard in the direction of the remaining carts, accompanied on the way by three delighted dogs. Two small carts stand side by side under the old cart-linhay. They are both of like pattern, but only one is sound and still in use, the other being broken in parts and lapsing into decay. We back the horse between the shafts of the former, hitch the back-chain, collar-chains and breeching, move out of the linhay and climb aboard. She rides like a boat, our little rail-cart, swaying with an easy motion as we go rattling down the rutty lane. The last of the Exmoor rail-carts she is—the last one whole and in use in all the country. In yards and linhays and strange odd corners of many a farm you will find her kindred, broken-wheeled and broken-railed, with the green stinging-nettles growing between the shafts and under the axle and tufts of grass among the boards. Soon our cart will go to join them, but for one more day at least she goes about a useful task.

These little harvest carts are of a type peculiar to the hill country of West Somerset, and not, I think, to be found anywhere else. Our cart is typical of the sort and may stand as a fair example for them all. She has the two wheels of an ordinary cart, but her body is that of a small wagon, long and narrow, slightly curved, and with low railed sides. The various parts are neatly chamfered and the rails smoothly turned. Lades are fixed fore and aft when required. Once the body was painted bright ultramarine blue with vermilion undercarriage, but now only a few vestiges of paint remain. A single horse between the shafts is usually sufficient for draught, but occasionally a chain-horse may be added for a heavy load on a long hill.

There is still something very attractive about our little cart—she seems in some way to combine something of the dignity of an ancient chariot with the grace of a boat, and she is well-balanced and easy to ride on and does not jolt like other carts. She turns or backs very easily on the two wheels, and her sort is well adapted to the sharp-angled turns of narrow gates and lanes and the steep hillsides of this rough country.

Now, today, as carts and horses are everywhere superseded by the powerful farm tractor, it is not easy to remember that once, not so very far beyond living memory, carts themselves were a modern and quite revolutionary innovation in this Exmoor country. Up to the beginning, and in many places almost to the middle of the last century, pack-horses were the sole means of transport on the lonely hill farms. Roads were non-existent, or at best hollow lanes and muddy moorland tracks, and all commodities—produce to market, peat home from the hill, manure up to the field—went in the swinging panniers of the pack-ponies. Withypool, in the district north-west of Dulverton, saw its first cart in the 1830's, when the then owner of the farm of Weatherslade, a certain Mr Quartly, bought a cart or wagon from somewhere in the lower country (Carhampton, I believe) and had it conveyed up to the hills. This cart arrived in Withypool, after its long and difficult journey, on a Sunday morning, and all the village turned out to see such a marvel.

A friend of mine tells me that an old lady of her acquaintance, now, alas, departed, used to recount to her the childhood memory of the arrival of the first cart in Exford. These were the days when the Church Hill was just a slippery bed of rock, and a perilous descent for anything with wheels. The date of this epoch-making event cannot have been much over a hundred years ago.

As an intermediary between pack-saddle and cart, a sledge or skid was sometimes used about the farms. I have never seen one myself, but these primitive things seem to have survived into quite recent times, for I have seen a photograph of such a sledge engaged in 'carting' peat up on the high moor. The thing seemed to be just a flat bed with some sort of low runners under it and a single horse attached.

Her errand done, our cart returns to the linhay and the horse to the stable. The throb of the tractor two fields away brings one's mind back to the present. The bawl of calves from the yard reminds one of other work.

Presently my way takes me over the fields and down the hills and out into a lane. How great is the contrast of the deep and sheltered lanes with the windy open space of the high fields and the moor! One seems to enter another country and another clime. I go slowly for the pleasure of all the joyful life around, and the image of summer that walks everywhere.

The lane is hot with the sun that is held between the high banks like a river of warmth. Underfoot the narrow road is dry and twists on, snakewise, deeper into the combe where the brook clatters and sings, until both meet together at the little grey bridge at the bottom.

The joy of a west-country lane in May! The high, close banks on either side are a garden of flowers in a terrace of sun, a hanging garden in a Babylon of grass, and all the way one goes a journey of delight into the midday province. Here are blue-bells, blue as sapphires, red campions, white stitchworts, delicate as stars, all intermingled, and all about them a thicket of young bronze-necked ferns. Here are speedwells like gentians, patches of yellow 'Welsh' poppies, tufts of yellow pimpernel, late primroses and violets, wild geraniums, lilac milkmaids, spikes of bugle, buttercups nearly as big as the poppies, and every-where pennyworts swelling and spiring up to the sun.

Bluebells and campions and white stitchworts and young green fern-fronds—a bunch of flowers that evoke the sound of the sea on a long jagged coast and the sun on the ocean's rim. The speedwells are too fragile to pick, but oh, what a blue they are! Each flower as it opens is a pure gentian blue—bluer than any other wild flower that I know—with a tiny eye of white in its centre. I do not know of what species it is, possibly quite a common one, but here it has a brilliance of blue like no other of its kind.

Above the flowers and ferns the sun shines through a glory of leaves and of blossom too. Delicate beech, orange-red sycamore like outstretched hands, green hazel and hawthorn, and ash just breaking from the bud. The snowfall of may-blossom falls from the thorn, and its heady scent drifts down the lane. Blue leaf-shadows dapple the roadway, and in the gutter a slow-worm slithers under the fringe of grass.

Now is the time that one might look for adders in odd woody or heathy places, but I have not seen an adder for these past ten years. Once they were very common in the rougher parts of the west country, and one would perhaps see several in the course of a single walk, but now they are seldom to be seen at all. A friend mentioned having come across one in her henyard one day this spring, but that is the only first-hand record I know of myself, though, by hearsay, one or two have been killed locally.

Lizards too, were at one time abundant and would frequently run across the sunny road like moving shadows before one's feet, but here again I have seen only one in the past decade. I do not know why our common reptiles should have become so scarce or so shy.

By the time I come home the blue tractor has finished its work for the day, and the big, three-furrow plough stands still and alone by the plough-field gate. I stop for a moment, held by the sudden beauty of the three gleaming silver shares— triple forms of curving light against the earth. How lovely they are, these things of forceful purposeful steel, polished by their voyage through the dark burnishing soil! how full of meaning and power and grace of accomplishment! The cleaving shares are the prows of Greek galleys, the shining mouldboards have the great curve of some piece of Missaglia armour. They are silver wings in the dusk of the hedge. I leave the plough to its sleep, and walk home across the fields to mine.

§

THE NOISY stream comes running hastily down the narrow valley to the ford, and here where it meets the lane it spills out into a wider, shallower pool, slackens for a moment to flow smoothly over the roadway, then gathers speed again to continue its tumbling way amongst rocks and stones and under hanging branches of alder and hazel and grey-leafed sallow. Here is a pleasant spot, a warm hollow in the valley, where white ducks from a cottage swim boat-like on the ford and where the sun, when it shines, is caught as though in a rounded bowl.

Beside the ford the little clapper footbridge strides across the water in three small leaps, giving dry footing to passers on the road and providing a point from which one can look both up and down the stream. The little bridge is a pleasing feature, and interesting too. The three clapper stones that compose its span are big slabs of old worn slate, some five feet or so in length and two feet or less in width, perhaps of a thickness of six inches, and are set up on small piers of lesser stones at a height that is just above the normal level of the running water. The water tumbles underneath from the smooth space of the ford to re-emerge on a rougher bed, and above is an iron handrail by which one can steady oneself when the stream is running high and threatening to break over the clappers.

One wonders when this useful little bridge was set here, and by whom. There is no clue to its age, but its stones must have been very heavy to move into position and would need a concerted effort of some sort, especially in the days before carts were in general use. Yet the difficulty of moving large slabs of heavy stone does not seem to have been in any way a deterrent to their use by former generations of moor folk, for great flags of slate are everywhere a feature of local construction, whether as gateposts, floor-slabbing, lintels or bridging. Certainly shale and slate is everywhere abundant on the moor, offering a plentiful building supply near to hand; so probably the builders did not have to go very far for their big stones in general, but from what—if any—particular quarries the very big dark blue flags come I do not know.

The prototype and arch-ancestor of all this megalithic tradition is the great clapper bridge of Tarr Steps, that crosses the Barle midway between Withypool and Dulverton. Here is one of the most splendid bridges of its kind in the whole country, with some twenty huge cyclopean blocks, upraised and buttressed by others of scarcely less size, striding across the broad swift-flowing river from side to side, most truly like the footstones of some mighty olden giant. It is said (though nothing is really known of its origin) to be the work of the Bronze Age men, of those same hands that raised the barrows and the circles and the strange forbidding Longstone. If this is so then one must wonder more at the mysteries of its construction than of any other stone thing on Exmoor, for the greatest of its blocks can surely only be measured in tons. How, and under whose authority, and for what specific reason such a work was erected in this one particular spot, by men whose only tools were of bronze and stone, and whose only motive power was that of their own limbs, and possibly those of oxen, is something one can only conjecture and muse about in the evenings when the river-wind rustles the leaves like a voice speaking and the water is full of shadows.

One's thoughts come back again to the little bridge. It has no great history like the mighty Tarr Steps, and may be not a hundred years old; yet it is in a direct line of descent, for within itself it carries the cylopean tradition down from the ages of prehistory into the use of modern times.

I lean on the iron rail awhile and look up the combe. A short distance off there are irritated calls, mewings and whistlings from the big ash tree that stands a little way up the slope, noisier today than I have heard them before. The buzzards have a nest high up in the ash, and now it seems they have a family as well. The buzzard as a protected bird has increased its numbers considerably in recent years, and one is seldom out of sight or sound of one or more of these splendid birds anywhere on the moor. Splendid indeed they are, soaring in space on great wings that spread almost motionless upon the air-current, gliding and wheeling so effortlessly above the hills. If the West Country had a crest it would surely be a buzzard *volant*. They are the biggest of our hawks, eagle-like in form, with their wide blunt wings and fingered pinions, but they do little harm to man's preserves, preying for the most part on nothing greater than rats and mice and young rabbits. The normal colouring of an adult buzzard is a chestnut brown, darkish on the upper parts and lightish on the breast, but there is a certain amount of variation amongst individual birds. I once saw a pure white buzzard. It was in April, on the Withypool side of the moor, on a bright clear day, and the beautiful wraith-like creature soared and wheeled against the blue sky, white as any gull. Only the very tips of its pinions were touched with dark colour as though marked with a pencil, and all the rest was snowy white. It was, I suppose, an albino, such as crops up in any family, human, bird or animal, on rare and unpredictable occasions.

But the fresh west wind comes eddying up the valley, stronger now, setting the leaf-laden trees hissing and surging under its ruffling fingers. Splatters of rain begin to fall from the darkening clouds. It is time to go. As I turn up over the fields the grass wipes wet about my feet, thick and green and damp with the promise of summer, and the soft, sweet rain closes in over the shortening afternoon and over the rising hills. From below and far off comes the soft murmur of the distant rivers and all the rushing streams, the water-sound, sister to the sea, the oldest sound in all the world. I stand again for a moment—then go slowly up the hill and away.

§

JUST WHERE our lane comes down the hill to meet the brook a white cottage stands with its garden by the road. A roof of thatch comes down to its windows, and its windows look back into the lane and over to the fields beyond. Across the milk-white walls and over the shallow porch pink roses trail and cluster, and at the foot bright borders of flowers make gay the roadside for a little way.

How sweet are the flowers here. Gentians big as thimbles and bluer than the bluest sky look up from amongst white anemones, tulips and wallflowers, red valerian, and a dozen different sorts of rock plants. Behind, at the end of the house, over the hedge, a patch of enclosed garden slopes towards the combe, brilliant with azaleas. Beyond, on the steep shoulders of the combe, the golden gorse flares amongst small, rough fields and a tangle of woods.

The place was once a holding, a small independent farmstead with perhaps twenty acres of ground and common rights on the moor that lies over the hill. Like so many of its sort, it has come on days that render it no longer an economic proposition in the agricultural sense, so its lands are let off and its dwelling now serves happily as a private residence. Still, though, one may see the mark of its former state in the little yard behind it, with stable and small shippon and what must have been once a pillared linhay flanking it about. Its thatch, like old velve above the green-painted windows, recall an earlier age when almost all farmhouses and their buildings were thatch-roofed, and only a few had slate, and none had known the indignity of tiles or composition. Thatch is undoubtedly the earliest and original moor roofing. There are few farms that do not retain some record or memory of thatch. About each one you will hear that the house, or this barn, or that shippon, was thatched 'in Grandfer's time'. Some Exmoor farmhouses still retain their thatch, but they are not many. Yealscombe and Higher Thorn in the parish of Exford, and Knighton in Withypool are three. Cloutsham on its lofty Ball was entirely thatched a generation ago. The criticism against thatch on the high moor is that it does not weather well in this predominantly wet and stormy climate, and for this reason it has always been replaced by slates whenever the owner could afford these. Such as still remains is now of wheat-reed, but in the olden days when rye was grown in the little fields rye-straw would have been used, and the thatch renewed and repaired as necessary with the home-produced reed. Rush out of the bogs was and still is used occasionally to thatch the little October corn ricks in the rick-splatt, but it is unlikely that bog-rush was ever used to roof the buildings.

Slate is the logical successor to thatch in these parts. The local rocks are slate-bearing and there are slaty outcrops in many places. The best slates in the district come from Treborough in the Brendons, where there were large and well-known quarry pits. These latter slates were very beautiful in colour and texture, being silvery and thick and with a roughish surface that weathered very pleasingly. Exmoor slates in general are big and very heavy—some of them are quite two feet square—and their colouring ranges from blue to silver. The brown pantiles that tend to prevail so much nowadays on the eastern side of the moor are a recent introduction of less than a hundred years' standing and, though not unsightly in appearance, have no natural tradition in the country. They are called, I believe, 'Bridgewater tiles', which term explains their origin explicitly enough.

The eye is drawn back to the flowers and the garden. How sweet a thing they are in the midst of moorland and rough country, how sweet a contrast, accentuating both themselves and the majesty of the wilderness. All dwellings hereabouts have their garden, a small irregular high-banked enclosure, set to face the sun, and often detached from the house itself like a tiny field; but these little 'plats' were intended for the mundane purpose of growing vegetables rather than for the cultivation of flowers, and flowers are not the general rule. But what a haven of delight can be created when one sets to making a flower garden and growing things for the pleasure of them. One must choose one's style of gardening and the plants to grow by the nature of the place, its prevailing soil and climate. The altitude here is high—most of the country lies over a thousand feet—and the soil predominantly acid and peaty, and the climate one of humidity, of rain and wild wind, but little real cold (that is, cold as judged by the standards of the eastern side of England). Our winters are usually open until after Christmas, and then frost, when it does come, is seldom deep enough to penetrate more than an inch or so into the ground. It is, I suppose, what one would call an Atlantic climate. Only in exceptional years does one get an icy winter.

The sort of garden that fits best into the natural order of things is one of rock garden type. Stone is everywhere abundant, raw and grey, and the soil is mostly thin, and there are few places that have not a little stream or splat of running water by them. Most of the ground is on a slope too. Retaining walls of dyking, slate-flag steps, paths of smooth cobbles from the river bed, some monolithic feature, perhaps a rill of fresh water running and falling over stones—great things can be attempted, and perhaps even done.

Grass grows here with a richness and depth of green that is perhaps unparalleled elsewhere outside of Ireland, for this is a natural grass country (which may at first seem strange on a naturally acid soil, but apparently other factors make up for the absence of lime content), so one must have grassy nooks and a small lawn. Large lawns, however, seem out of place in this country of ups and downs and little enclosures.

As to flowers, what shall one choose, what grows best in this hill country? First of all, the heaths and heathers—for their kind are native-born all around. Of these there are many beautiful sorts, both natural and cultivated, and with good

63

judgment and careful planting one may have heather in bloom nearly all the year round. Then there are the alpines, most of which naturalize well, especially gentians, and fit nicely into a rocky setting. Of the larger shrubs, azaleas are best of all, delighting as they do in the peaty lime-free soil—and what a glory of colour they make in the early months of summer! Brooms too flourish well, as is natural, they being of the gorse family. Roses grow tolerably well, and put up quite a good show. Primulas and spring bulbs of all sorts seem also to do well, though the wild daffodil does not grow in our valleys. Most annuals will flourish and grow easily in the lightish soil.

In passing it is to be noted that apple trees do not grow upon Exmoor—the wild crab is not to be found anywhere; neither will cultivated apples prosper.

Back home once more I settle down for the evening. The clouds tonight are gathering for one of those great twilight cloudscapes that present themselves from time to time above the moor. The sun has gone, and now through the open window there is only the illimitable space of the western sky, pale luminous yellow, with the dark evening clouds marching along the horizon. Like black giants they tower up from the rim of the moor, ever changing forms, wondrous, terrible, dark shapes passing across the face of the infinite. I reach out my hand and turn on the wireless. The great passages of the last movement of Beethoven's Fifth Symphony fill my room, and the glorious music rises and falls and swells and reaches out in a greater harmony to the sky and the clouds, triumphant and exultant as though a soul were ascending into heaven. As the final majestic chords die away the clouds sink and pass into night and silence. For a while the twilight glow lingers on the horizon, and then that too fades into the night.

June

ON THE little patch of close-bitten turf by the lip of the bog the ponies idle in the morning sun.

Now is the fullness of the year for them. Fresh green grass in abundance, sunny days and soft nights, peace and plenty. The cold winds of winter and the bitter searching for sustenance are forgotten. Now every mare has her foal at foot. Overhead the larks sing in joyous space, and all about the bog the yellow water-buttercups and turquoise forget-me-nots make a gay tapestry amongst the tufted rushes. Only a few sheep stir in the nearby heather to disturb the sleepiness of midday. Only a soft southerly breeze like a breath ruffles the warm air.

Like a garland the ponies are cast on the grass, some standing, or grazing, idly swinging their shining tails, some lying down, a few sprawled headlong on the smooth turf. Resplendent in their new summer coats, they have changed much since winter. The sun shines with brassy gloss on the sheen of their polished bodies. The short fine coats of the mares are a bright rich colour, bay or brown, and the mealy underparts have deepened to a dusky tan. The mealy noses too are less distinct, the bay-brown colour extending now almost to the black nostrils. Their black points look indigo blue in the light. The yearlings, though, are still to be distinguished by their generally lighter colour, with the mealiness of the underparts still pronounced.

The foals, most of them no more than a week or two old, or even less, are little light-coloured things of rough mealy coat and awkward gangling legs. Already, though, their backs and faces are darkened to red or brown, and each has the flour-white nose and black nostrils of its race. The little brush tails and short upright manes are mostly sooty black, though a few are as yet silvery-coloured.

Some of the older foals play together, experimenting with their new-found legs, or nose at the bright saucers of water amongst the rushes, or nibble at blades of grass. They flick furry ears at slight sounds, and look with the wonder of youth at every strange and mysterious thing.

On the edge of the herd the stallion grazes, his thick mane falling on both sides of his neck and his long tail lazily flicking at a few odd flies. Now and again he raises his head and crested neck to survey his kingdom, alert beneath his apparent somnolence for any alien footstep or anything that might threaten the wellbeing of his herd. Occasionally one or other of the foals will sidle up to him and nibble at his face or tail, all of which he takes in good part.

Once again one's eyes are drawn to the foals. They are so like many of the little horses of the palaeolithic pictures, and so vital and alive. Their baby heads accentuate the triangular face of their kind with the broad forehead, deep jaw and eye set low in the face, while the white belly and darker back are the colouring of the wild. Perhaps all the horses were coloured thus

67

once, for it is often said that the very young mirror the appearance of the parent race in former ages. Apropros of this I once saw an Exmoor foal that was striped all over at birth like a young zebra. The little creature was the usual mealy colour, but its head, neck and forearms, and body from shoulder to buttock, were overlaid with a network of fine brownish stripes. The mane and tail were silvery. This peculiar marking was most pronounced from birth to the age of one week. Thereafter the stripes faded quickly, or more precisely fused together, so that in a very short while the foal was a normal brown-mealy colour. Both dam and sire were registered Exmoors, the one brown and the other dark bay, and the filly foal—for such it was—grew up to be a handsome young mare of dark brown colour with black points, her mane and tail having turned quite black by the second year.

I wander on across the moor. Already the first pink bells of *Erica tetralix* are opening in the sun—the heather will be early this year—and the little yellow dragon-mouths of the cow-wheat rise from the green mat. Cloudy trails of white woodruff run everywhere, mocking the heather. In the hollows amidst the rushes little pools reflect the sky with rippling blue, and from one a heron rises as I pass, his great arched wings of white and grey majestic in the sunlight.

Presently I turn into a lane, or rather a roadway that has grass verges on either hand and low heather-matted banks beyond. Here, unbitten by stock, the grass grows high in all the glory of full growth, as though it had been planted especially to give delight to passers-by. So lovely it is, rippling and shining in the breeze, gold and silver, green and bronze, purple and pink and cream-coloured. Sweet-vernal, bent and fescue, tall hair-grass and soft-grass, rushes tasselled like Saracen lances and perhaps a dozen other sorts whose names I barely know. How infinitely beautiful is grass, the most vital and least-thought-of plant in all the world. With what wondrous grace it grows and flowers, with what liberality it covers the earth, with what generosity it feeds the beasts of the field and their master, man. 'There is no flesh but grass.' It is truly said. If we did but give praise where it is due, it is the good green blades that should be our emblem of life, and the delicate flowering heads the objects of our homage.

The day is a delight, and all things a vision, but I go home early, for I have promised to 'see sheep' tonight, and so must not fail to do this. Each week, each day now, that leads up to shearing, is one of constant worry and anxiety for the sheep farmer, for as the wool gets heavier so the sheep get more desirous of rolling, and the more helpless when they do so. A heavy-woolled sheep over on its back cannot get up: it just stiffens and dies unless aid comes in time. Many farmers set up sticks or stones or drag old carts into the fields to serve as 'scratchers' for the sheep in the hope of dissuading them from rolling, but always there are losses just the same, no matter how careful one is. The most dangerous time would seem to be an interval of warm sun after rain, for then the creatures are seized with a great urge to roll—no doubt because the drying of their fleeces causes their backs to itch—with the usual fatal results. The length of time a sheep will live while on its back varies. Some will die in little more than half an hour, others will linger for several hours. Probably a good deal depends on how heavily a sheep has filled its stomach prior to going over, and possibly something is owed to the constitution of the individual sheep itself.

Alas, it is all just another of the worries and hazards, of which there are many, of sheep farming in the hills.

§

ALONG THE banks of the narrow lane the foxgloves tower above the brushing ferns, rank upon rank of tall rose-colour spires pointing up to the blueness of the sky and the white summer clouds, and throwing back thin shadows to the dry, dusty roadway. All about them the green ferns, stretched to the fullness of growth, reach out with feathery fronds from the great tufts, rooted between the earth and stone, filling the lane with the warm sweet fragrance that is like no other thing. Ferns and foxgloves! How they evoke the spirit of the dear West Country, and all one's memories of it.

Dear rose-purple foxgloves. How joyously they grow—six feet tall if they can, and more—in all odd places, and thick as grass on the tops of fresh-laid banks. Wherever a hedge is laid they spring up in masses to claim lordship in the sunshine where they may, before they are ousted again by the resurgent beech, and they dispute many an odd corner with the rapacious bracken, and even take root amongst the heather and edge the moorland streams with spires. Their clanging colour shouts to the blue and green of the summer, and tosses over the banks to the heady meadows deep in grass and cries midsummer all the way.

What of the ferns? They are the green glory of the western lanes. They love the damp weather, the sun of the morning, the deep shadow of the bank in the afternoon. They mass themselves in tropic confusion wherever the site is pleasing to themselves, and grow, should conditions be favourable, to immense size and stature. In one place I know there are great clumps of common-fern as tall as I am and thick-round at the root like a tree. Where luxury is wanting they still contrive to grow, though with diminished size. And what a variety of sorts one may find in different parts of one lane. Here in the sunnier parts the big 'common' or 'male' fern and the even bigger but more delicate lady-fern and buckler-fern predominate. In damper and shadier spots the long smooth ribbons of the hart's-tongue droop down. In woody places the hard-fern and the polypody jostle for places, the latter often taking up residence in the root-stocks of the beech itself. Where there is old walling you will find the pretty little maidenhair-spleenwort, the black-spleenwort and the tiny wall-rue. In some walls the rusty-back grows, but as this little fern has a liking for lime, in which the country is generally deficient, it tends to reside only in those walls in which lime-plaster has been used.

These ferns are by no means all that are to be found on and about the fern country of the west, but they are all that I am willing to list, as intermediary fern species in excess of these are difficult for a layman to identify with certainty. There are several sorts of medium-sized ferns that grow amongst the heather, one of which is probably the lemon-fern. Some previously known ferns have become extinct, or practically so. The oak-fern is said to have resided in the rocks above Landacre Bridge not so very long ago, but I have not seen it, though I know the place well. There are records of the genuine maiden-hair-fern having existed in places on the western side of the moor in the last century, but it was probably exterminated by ruthless collectors a long while ago. Likewise the great royal-fern *Osmunda* is no longer to be found, though I believe it used to exist. The parsley-fern used to live on Exmoor, and may still do so, but again I have never seen it, or cannot say with certainty that I have.

The reverie on ferns is broken abruptly by the advent of a large lorry coming up the lane. We come face to face, and it stops. Its sides touch the ferny banks both left and right, and there is not a passage for the smallest creature. There is nothing for it but to scramble ingloriously up the bank, which I do, and perching somewhere near the top amongst the foxgloves, wave the driver on. We both laugh. Such are the hill country byways.

Our Exmoor lanes are deep and narrow, scored to bedrock below the level of the flanking fields, sunny canyons when the top growth is laid back, shadowy tunnels where the hedges meet overhead, steep and twisting for most of their way and lit like corridors with narrow gates. Down them in rough weather the rains and spilling springs come pouring, as down a river bed, tearing at the roadway surface and swilling mud and debris all the way.

Some are blessed with tarmac now, some have only the rammed stone 'metal' still for a surface, just two wheel tracks with a mat of grass between, on which one can canter a horse, while others have no surface at all, only clattering stones, raw slippery rock and pools of splashing mud. Even the best of them find little favour with the drivers of modern vehicles, and traffic to and from some of the lonelier farms is frequently something of a problem in this day and age of motor-lorries and huge top-heavy cattle-trucks. In some even a horse and cart will brush the ferny banks, so narrow are they, and often the gradient is frightening.

Our lanes and tracks were never made for wheeled vehicles of any sort. They are horsemen's roads, pack-horse ways, scored out of the brown or peaty earth long before the first cart ever came westwards into Exmoor country. The earliest farm carts came into the region in or about the 1830's, and prior to this the only and indigenous method of transport was that of the sturdy pack-horse. The roads of olden times were made for the feet of trotting ponies, scored to the rock where possible for safe footing, hollow and U-shaped, just wide enough for the swinging panniers to pass the banks. All things went by pack-pony—merchandise from the townships, produce to market, lime from the kiln, manure to the fields, corn to the barn. Summer and winter, in all weathers, the ponies splashed through the fords and rattled over the little bridges, nine in a string, their packs swaying and bells ringing, on their way from farm to farm and to the outer world.

Little documentary evidence exists concerning the pack-ponies of Exmoor, but every farm would have its string and the various sorts of tackle necessary thereto. For transporting bulky stuff some sort of pack-saddle would be used, whilst for 'carting' manure, panniers with pegged bottoms are known to have been used—the ponies would plod up the steep fields with their loads of muck from the yard, and then at the appropriate spot the pins would be pulled out and the load let drop through the flap-bottoms to fall to the ground in two little heaps. An elderly friend, who as a girl used to visit a farm in the Withypool district, once told me that she could remember seeing the pile of old pack-horse tackle mouldering in one of the tallets. What happened to this museum stuff, I wonder? Probably it went on a bonfire when someone got around to tidying up the tallet.

As to the pack-ponies themselves, it seems most probable that they were just the larger-grown Exmoors of the district, or a cross therefrom. (The Exmoor pony is capable of carrying a tremendous weight for its size, as anyone can witness who has seen a 12-hand pony carrying a very heavy rider.) At one time the Devonshire pack-horse was a well-known animal in the West Country, but like the hunter it seems to have been a type rather than a breed, and here again its foundation was Exmoor or Dartmoor mares crossed with something larger to give it extra size and substance.

In passing it is only fair to say that some of the Exmoor roads are very good indeed, broad and spacious with grass verges on either hand. These, however, would have been made in com-paratively recent times, probably about the beginning of the last century when so much of the common land and open moor was enclosed under the various Enclosure Acts. Sometimes, too, after the general introduction of wheeled vehicles an ancient highway was completely remade, and in certain places one may still see the old lane—a deep sunken U-shaped hollow—

running parallel to the new wide tarmac road. A good example of this is the main road into Exford from Chibbet Post.

§

SUN, SHADOW and a sou'west wind. Here I sit on the lonely barrow, set in the midst of the sea of sedge, with the sky like a bowl coming down to the horizon all round. North and south, east and west, the morass of bog laps unbroken about the barrow, about this one spot of sound ground in all the welter of sogging liquid peat. Here is the heart of the Forest; here are desolation and emptiness. Here are silence and loneliness. Even the sky is empty, for neither raven nor buzzard quarters this preyless waste. Solitude, utter and complete.

As I sit on the sunward side of the barrow under the blowing breeze, I can just see, afar off, the summit of Exe Head, blue above the rim of sedge, and beyond, farther still, the head of Dunkery like a small smudge of cloud under the sky. That is all of the outer world beyond the great bog, and it is no different from the clouds. It might almost be a landscape from the moon, or some planet untrodden by man rather than a piece of our own country. It is as a world unformed, a land in the making, holding still the grandeur of desolation.

But now I must arise and go, retracing my uneasy steps by the way that I came. The going is slow. I tread from tussock to tussock of the short tufted deer-sedge, avoiding with care the thick mats of sphagnum moss that spread around in blotches of sinister yellow, coiling snake-like amongst the sedge. All beneath is the treacherous peat, black, oozing and seemingly bottomless. Here and there, thrusting up through the sedge and moss, are the lilac-purple heads of small spotted orchis, strangely exotic in such company. The ground for a moment seems even more spongy and uncertain; I thrust my stick into the mat to test it; the stick goes in up to the grip—goodness knows how deep is the morass. I veer my course a little and keep more carefully to the sedge.

Now the deer-sedge gives way to billowing stretches of cotton-grass. Acre upon acre of shining silver-white heads in the sun, as far as the eye can see, white like a summer snowfall. It is lovely. One's eyes rejoice in all the silvery, silky brightness and nodding beauty. There are two species, I note, that make up the snowy expanse—the single-headed Hare's Foot or Hare's Tail (*Eriophorum vaginatum*) and the so-called Common Cotton-grass (*E. augusticolium*); but it is the Hare's Tail that predominates.

I make heavy going of the way through the white cotton-grass, but at length, after a mile or so, the ground becomes firmer as I come gradually down to lower ground, and the cotton-grass dissolves into the ascending tide of bent and moor-grass. Here suddenly are cattle, hock-deep in the mingled rush and bent and cotton-grass, massive black beasts that lift weird white faces from the grass to stare at me. They are Galloway-cross-Hereford, a type of beast that seems to do well on the high moor, combining the hardiness of the Galloway stock with heavier beef of the Hereford. They have the polled heads of the Galloway still, and at their feet are red and white calves that must be from a second Hereford cross. They are impressive, and a fine sight against the sky with the rough grass up to their bellies.

Through a gate in a boundary fence and up the flank of another hill, and I sit down again in the tussocky grass for a rest. The hills rise and fall all round in undulating flow like the running sea, tawny with bent and sedge, blanketed with bog on the heights, threaded with narrow peaty streams in the hollows. This is the Forest, the inner heart of Exmoor, the last wilderness of the ancient land. Here is no heather, no tree, no scrub—only loneliness and space. Why, one asks oneself, should this empty land be called a Forest? The answer is that the word 'forest' as applied by medieval usage was a judicial term, not a botanical one. In ancient times a forest was an area of land held by the Crown as a royal hunting-ground, subject to forest law, and approximating in general character to what we would now call a game reserve. It had no direct association with trees, though the fact that many forests—such as Sherwood and the Hampshire New Forest—were heavily wooded may have caused the words woodland and forest to become synonymous in general usage. Such forests as Exmoor and Dartmoor never had any trees upon their heights.

When, at what date, wild Exmoor was claimed as a royal

hunting-ground is uncertain, but as it was already so before the Norman Conquest, this must have happened some time in the days of the Saxon or Anglo-Danish kings. Why it was claimed is more easily answered; from time immemorial the West Country in general and the combes and heights of Exmoor in particular have been the harbour of the wild red deer that were ever the royal prey of kings. The kings of England, of whatever dynasty, made little bones of securing for themselves the chief haunts of the deer. We know, anyway, that in early days Exmoor Forest included not only the inner area we now know as the Forest but almost all of the whole moorland district with all its deep combes and thick deer coverts of scrub-oak. Gradually it seems that the Crown was made to disgorge much of outer Exmoor, so that by the fourteenth century the Forest consisted only of the desolate inner waste we know by that name today.

As the extent of the Forest shrank to the area of grassy, boggy, windswept height and the greater deer coverts were lost to it, its value to the Crown became less that of a hunting preserve and more and more that of a huge pastoral grazing ground. Throughout the long Middle Ages and right up to the first years of the nineteenth century great herds of cattle and flocks of sheep, and horses too, were driven up every spring from the surrounding commons and moor farms to summer pasture on the high Forest. For this valuable privilege all had to pay a certain fixed price per head of stock, all that is except the farmers of Withypool and Hawkridge. These, the holders of the fifty-two free suit tenements of the aforesaid parishes, had the peculiar right to dispasture their stock free of charge upon the Forest, and to hold various other rights there as well, but in return for these privileges they had certain duties and obligations to fulfil when called upon.

The rights of the free suitors were, I believe, identical with those rights enjoyed by them upon their own commons. Their duties seems to have consisted mainly of an obligation to 'drive' the Forest, upon horseback, a number of times a year for the necessary rounding-up of livestock, and to attend in person the annual courts or 'swainmotes' at which the affairs of the Forest were decided and various disputes settled.

How the men of Withypool and Hawkridge, and they alone, came to possess these rights, and be so bound with the Royal

Forest, is unknown. All that can be said is that the custom of the free suitors had existed from time out of mind until the disafforestation of 1914. Withypool itself was always closely associated with the Forest and was, until the establishment of Simonsbath in the seventeenth century, more or less the centre of adminstration for Forest affairs. Before the founding of Simonsbath farm in the middle of the Forest, during the Commonwealth period when the Forest was leased to a private landowner, there had been no building of any sort within the bounds of the Forest, nor was there any other until after the disafforestation.

The pastoral days of high Exmoor lasted until the opening years of the nineteenth century, when the Crown finally decided to relinquish its ownership of Exmoor Forest, and an Act was passed for the disafforestation and sale thereof. After various allotments had been made in compensation of those who lost various rights and interests, and after all the livestock had been driven down from the heights for the last time, Exmoor Forest was offered for sale by tender to the highest bidder. One John Knight, a man of great pioneering spirit, bought the huge empty expanse, and he, together with his son Frederick, joined battle with the moor, and fought it for many years. Between them they carved some thirteen fine farms from the waste, and made roads where aforetime there had been nothing but muddy horsemen's tracks amongst the rushes, but in the end they never really tamed the Forest. The gale-swept, bog-blanketed heights still remain as they ever were, a last stronghold of sullen nature defiant against man.

So here is the high Forest still, sullen, treeless, rain-soaked, shrouded in mist for many of its days, yellow like a prairie for most of the year, grey-green with fresh growth for just a few weeks about midsummer, known in its inner parts to few save huntsmen and shepherds on horseback, and tenanted only by sheep and cattle and the deer that harbour in the fern.

One thing that has frequently called for comment, and a subject on which one must often ponder oneself, is the general absence of heather within the Forest. All around the bounds the encircling commons of Exmoor are thickly grown with heather—'black ground' as we say—yet once within the Forest area the heath comes more or less to a sudden end, giving way entirely to 'green moor'. Now the question that one asks is whether this distinction is entirely natural or induced. Myself, I am inclined to think that the order of things is a natural one, though subsidiary influences may have accentuated the difference. Firstly, the area of the Forest comprises that region of the moor which receives the highest rainfall and is most exposed to the prevailing Atlantic weather, and which on its heights is predominantly bogland. Heather, though it consents to grow on most wet peaty ground, is by no means a lover of the excessively wet and extremely acid conditions such as prevail over much of the high land, and it seems likely the Forest bounds as we know them happen to coincide with the natural limits to which the heather is prepared to colonize the western heights. Secondly, though it is well known that different methods of grazing and land management can alter the vegetation of given areas out of all recognition, there is nothing in the history of the Forest or commons to suggest that the general management and stocking of either differed radically from the other in any way in the past. Summer stocking, winter withdrawal and spring swaling seem to have been observed equally in all parts. The only point at which man could have been an interfering agent in the natural ecology of the Forest might have been in the time of the Knights, when the newly enclosed farmlands were heavily limed, and some lime may have been cast on the wilder parts. Heather is a hater of lime; but even so I cannot believe that this could have been sufficient to alter radically the natural character of so large an area of land.

The distinction set forth, however, is not entirely absolute. There is some heather within the Forest bounds, and there are areas of 'grass moor' outside. By and large, though, the vegetation of the high forest consists almost entirely of moor grasses (mostly *Molinia* and *Agrostis*), cotton grass (*Eriophorum*), rush (*Juncus*), sedges (*Carex*) and, on the highest bogs, deer-sedge or deer-grass (*Scirpus cespitosus*). There is also bracken on the lower slopes.

As one feels the afternoon slide away and the twilight—even the warm dusk of a summer's evening—come nearer, one hurries, glad to be down off the heights before the sun is gone. After sundown all the loneliness and solitude of the Forest are intensified into a strange inhumanity—a hostility almost—as though the spirit of the sullen earth drew resentfully away from man in this last and unassailed stronghold of the wilderness. The rough heather ground, the woods in the tangled bottoms, the little fields that lap round the farms, alike seem friendly after the desolation of the hills above. One feels the hedges close around one as a child feels the walls of its nursery, known and familiar. The smell of wood smoke from an unseen chimney, sweet and stirring, draws one on, beckoning to tiring footsteps, and once again one is home in the world of men.

§

THIS MORNING the air is full of the sound of sheep on the move. All about the low grey farm and over the fields and down the valley the sound of their bleating carries on the west wind to tell the world of another shearing. The midsummer sun shines gloriously, with only a few fair-weather clouds in the sky, and there is no threat of rain to hold up the work.

Down in the yards all is noise and bustle, as the wild-eyed hill sheep are driven by shouting men and barking dogs in from the lane and into the pens and dark buildings floored with oat-straw and green nettles. They come fearfully, these horned sheep of the moor, suspiciously, ready to break and wheel from the ring of men and dogs and leap up and over the surrounding banks. Their fleeces, dust-coloured from the weather, are so thick that their squat faces are quite covered with wool, and they seem as broad as they are long. The weight of their wool, though, does not impede their movement. They bunch at the dark open doors, and then first one and then another will twist and run like a goat, only to be brought back by the dog, until, overwhelmed by human insistence, they pour in sheer panic into the darkness within. Ewes call desperately to lambs parted from them in the housing, and lambs bawl for lost mothers; but here they must bide until their turn comes to be hustled over to the shearing barn.

At last the day's work is well under way. The shearing barn under the beeches is full of noise and rhythmic energy—the chugging of the engine, the throbbing vibration of the building, the whirring of the clippers, the bleating of sheep. Across the middle of the floor where the tackle runs the shearers stand, working rhythmically and unceasingly. Their lean bodies and brawny arms move with a steady calculated action, stooping or straightening, holding and turning the mesmerized sheep, while all the while their right hands sweep with unerring purpose. Their rhythm is broken only when they release a shorn sheep and reach out to take another. Before them, at the darker end of the barn, the heavy-woolled sheep stand in a close-pressed mass in the catching-pen, waiting like sacrificial beasts before an altar. Behind the shearers a white-coated tier takes the fleeces as they fall, and spreads, folds and ties them, throwing them up in an ever-mounting pile in the racks against the walls. Self and assistant catch out one sheep after another from the pen and bring them struggling to the shearing-board. Someone wields a broom, sweeping back to the scatterings of sawdust into the pen. Another hand stamps shorn beasts afresh with the blue marking-paint as they leave the barn, blazoning them with the cipher of ownership. The pungent smells of hot sheep, machine-oil, fresh wool and oily marking-paint—all mingle together and blend with the noise and movement.

All the while the heavy fleeces fall away from the sheep like cloaks on to the shearing-board, one after the other, milk-white curdled with a rich creamy-yellow yoke, like foam from the sea. Shorn sheep emerge goat-like, white spectres of their former selves, bewildered, and scarcely able to gather their wits together for the run to freedom. So it goes on, sheep after sheep —first the hoggs, then the ewes and lambs together, and then there will be the rams to finish with. For the hill farmer it is the first harvest of the year.

Dinner time, and the machinery stops in a pool of silence. Out from the barn one steps into the glory of the midsummer world, half dazzled by the brilliance of the light, with the sunshine hot on one's face and hands. Blue sky and white clouds soar above green trees tossing in the breeze. Foxgloves cling to the banks, their rose-colour spires nodding over tall waving grasses. The hedges are heavy with elder-flower. The splat runs sparkling over the dry lane and down by the rocks, and the trunks of the tall beech trees stand silver under the heavy foliage, sculptured in the strong light of the sun, spilling indigo shadow into the yard. Beyond the heady fields I can see the moor stretching itself blue and gold under the midday sky.

The shearing dinner, with its turkey and ham on huge dishes, and bowls of sugared strawberries and cream, and its gossiping good fellowship, is over all too quickly. Again the engine starts to chug and rattle, and the men resume their work. The little field beside the barn fills more and more with shorn white bodies, and with much confusion bleating ewes and lambs sort themselves out into families again. How quickly a sheep is sheared with the mechanical clippers. It must have been an infinitely long and laborious job to shear a large flock in the days when hand-shears were the only instruments. The average Exmoor clips out at between five and six pounds and the Closewool at about seven pounds, but the fleeces of the rams are much heavier.

The sun is in the west when the engine stops again. This time work is over for the day, and the shearers collect their belongings to go home, while the rest of us drive our shorn flocks back up the lane to the various fields. They are like creatures of another species, these leggy, goat-headed creatures, no longer like sheep at all, so different are they from their former selves who came down to the yards this morning At least we shall have no more trouble with ewes over on their backs for a while now.

Tomorrow we shall shear the Closewools and the Dorsets, and then the shearing will be done for the year. One more day, and the worry over the heavy-woolled creatures will be finished.

The sun touches the horizon and the long warm summer twlight stretches out over the fields full of white sheep grazing at peace. How fortunate we are in having these days of fine dry weather for our shearing week. How different a tale it is when rain sets in, and the work has to stop, or cannot begin at all—for one cannot shear wet fleeces—and every day is a wretchedness of waiting, with all the while the constant danger of more losses from rolling. Yes, indeed we have had good luck this year.

§

THE SUN floods straight down from above with the strong overhead light of midsummer. Our fields lie lazing in the sunshine, deep with grass, and the trees heavy with the fullness of leaf sweep down to meet them. The sweet scent of white clover suffuses everything. The tall mowing grass is sheened with bronze, all heady and thick, and the meadows are dappled with flowers. Along the banks the hawkweeds are golden suns, standing out from the grassy walls on thin, dark, almost invisible stalks so that they seem to float like a hovering golden galaxy. Over everything is warmth and light, and under the hedges the sheep, white from the shearing like figures cut from new ivory, seek the shade away from the hot noonday sun.

Under a favourite bank I throw myself down for a moment and lie in the grass to drink in this idyll of summer. The grass is a shining jungle all around me now, and the flowers exotic wonders, and the sky curves down to me through the grass heads. My bank above me has a counterpoint of little yellow tormentils and white woodruffs under the flaunting hawkweeds, and tall rose-red spires of foxgloves reach up to meet majestic beech hardening now to summer gloss. The sun is hot and the smell of the clover intoxicating. Afar off I can just see the backs of the grazing horses monstrous above the grass head.

Fields! How great is the personality of a field. A piece of ground, a patch of precious earth, surrounded by four hedges that make of it a room open to the sky and all the moods of heaven. No one field is ever quite like another. Each has its own character, each its own aspects, its own individuality. Each becomes to one who treads often therein a place of being, intimately interwoven with one's self, a place of thoughts and memories, of moods and happenings and associations.

Man long ago recognized the reality of fields in those first days when he gave them names as he would a beast or a friend or some familiar object. All our fields have names: Pullen, Cherry, Blacketts, Gutterfield, Three Corners, Sally's, Big Cleeve, Twelve Acres, Horsefield, Cowfield, Square Meadow, Old Ground, Head Down, Dry Mead, Ferny Field, Yettypiece, New Ground, Gwanafield, Pennyfield, Broad Close, Studlands, Higher Leys, Lower Leys, Gratton, Dipford, Daisyfield. How and why and when the fields were christened is a thing to muse about. Every name must have had a meaning once, an allusion or a commemoration. Some of them are obvious, others may be guessed at, but some remain forgotten for all time.

Our fields are mostly small according to general standards.

The average Exmoor field is about five acres in extent, more or less, though some may be a bit bigger and many much smaller. The biggest field in our parish is our Twelve Acres, which is exceptionally large for the district. In general, the older the fields are the smaller they are. The little irregular plats of an acre or so that lie close to the farms probably represent the oldest enclosures made, set out when first the farms were settled perhaps 700 or even 1,000 years ago. In those days a man would not take in more ground at a time than he could cope with in a season. Bigger fields came later, when agricultural techniques improved, and some very large enclosures do exist out towards the Forest, which represent the wholesale enclosure of open moor during the eighteenth and nineteenth centuries.

All our fields are hedged about with the high earthen banks, and our gateways are narrow, often very narrow indeed. Seven feet, or even six, is a fair enough width between the posts of many of the older gates, and few exceed nine feet. Those that do may be assumed to be of fairly recent making, or later altera-tion. All that was required in the way of width in early times was just enough space for the panniers of the pack-ponies to swing through the gateways. The gates themselves have always been of simple pattern, five bars and a single or two uprights, and a diagonal, but it is surprising what a variation there can be on this one traditional theme, and few gates seem quite alike. Gateposts are usually just two stout logs of oak, but monolithic slabs of moorstone are not uncommon. The coigns of the thick banks behind the posts are rounded, and mostly faced with stone dyking.

The long afternoon stretches out till the sun begins to lower in the west. The shadows grow longer on the flowery grass and the white sheep turn to golden images, mirrored in blue.

Midsummer Night's Eve. Now is the culmination of a week of the most beautiful nights I have ever known. Again the sun sinks in glory to a cloudless horizon, and every head of grass stands shining in the western light as though the fields were the courts of heaven. As the hotness of the sun's breath is withdrawn the whole air is filled with the scent of the cooling beech leaves and every green thing, a scent like green apples, like sweetbrier, a green smell that is like the life of every growing thing loosed on the evening. It pervades the earth and comes to one in waves as one approaches the tall beech hedges, filling one with thoughts that are wordless.

The sun drops behind the hedges leaving a golden space of pure light, and the hedges turn dark and black between the realms of earth and sky. Over the tall flowering grasses big white moths hover like innumerable ghosts, insubstantial as fragments from a dream. The golden glow slowly sinks, and fades to a mystic pervading green, the green twilight of the midsummer hills. It will last all night, or almost so, for at midnight you will still see the green glow right in the north where the sun lies not far below the earth's rim. The still-shining sea of grass seems to reach towards me, and brushes tall against my knees, and over my shoulder a nightingale sings somewhere in the dark hedge close at hand. It is pure magic. A midsummer night's dream indeed.

I turn away at last from this waking dream and retrace my steps, for I have still some odd jobs to do, one of which is to burn up a bit of rubbish. Home now, I light my fire, and as the flame leaps up from the twilight earth to the sky, touching the leaves around with points of light, I remember that once men lit ritual fires on this shortest summer night in praise of the sun and the fullness of the year and hope for the following harvest. Flame in the twilight. It is so elemental a thing. My little fire leaps high. It stirs things so very deep and old beyond explaining. Is it some primeval memory of camp fires long ago? I don't know, but it is beautiful and cruel, the burning fire, friend and foe in one, consuming like a heart turned upon itself.

The flames die down, and for a while the world is dark after the fiery light of them. Then the luminous midsummer twilight reasserts itself, and the land moves under the green heavens silently towards midnight.

July

As I come up over the brow of the moor, there, suddenly
before me, over the head of the green, deep bracken, five golden
beasts stand in the sun like fabled creatures from the dawn of
the world. Deer! I drop into the bracken at once and am still.
They have seen me, but just for a moment they hesitate, looking
in my direction, compelled by curiosity to linger. They are five
hinds all in the shining splendour of their new summer coats,
polished and red-gold in the morning light. Just for that
moment they look at me with wide ears pricked and heads held
high on the long snake necks, and then they are gone, disappeared as suddenly and completely as imagined creatures.

They must have fled down some hidden goyal, for there is no sign of them as I rise up and look about. No doubt they have young calves tucked away somewhere down under the cover of fern in the lonely valley.

How one's heart leaps at the sight of the wild red deer! No fat and placid park deer, however beautiful, can rouse the same emotion, even though they be of the same species. It is the creatures of the wild that excite, that stir forgotten depths within us, that make the pulse beat in the wrists. Perhaps it is the essential freedom of the creature, the pride, the independence of it, living outside and in defiance of man's world that arouse one's admiration, perhaps just the grace and alertness of the wild that are ever lost in domestication, perhaps because deep within one the atavistic instincts stir with memories of a world in which all things were wild, and man a hunter for his meat. Whatever the answer might be, there are few things left in this land that thrill like the sight of wild deer in the bracken on a hillside in summer.

These, our red deer of the hill and combe, are truly wild, indigenous beasts of the brake and shadowy oak wood of the west, beasts whose forbears trod with slender cloven hoof the same wet earth as the untamed ox and wolf and little fleeing horse. Their red coats shone in the morning sun before ever a man set axe to a tree or laid a stone for a lonely cot between the forest and heathery hill, and their antlers spired to the sky when wild boar crashed in the undergrowth and metal ore slept in the dark in the untilled earth. Once they roamed the length and breadth of all the land of Britain, but now life and man have driven them back from all their ancient kingdom, save for the hills of the west where the wooded combes run down to the sea and the lordship of the wild is not yet broken. Here, in the remote and windswept fastness of Exmoor, the wild deer have survived, whilst in all other parts the race has long departed, leaving only a few emparked remnants to remind us that Britain too once had great game equal to any in the world. Nowhere else in the south of England but in Devon and Somerset do the truly indigenous wild deer remain, and many weary miles separate them from their northern kindred.

That the wild red deer, *Cervus elaphus*, should indeed have survived through the centuries and into this day and age in the

face of all the advancing tides of civilization, and in so circumscribed an area, is truly something to marvel at. Even granting
the remoteness of the Exmoor country from the general tide of
affairs, and its natural wildness, this fact alone is not a complete
explanation for the continued existence of so fine a wild
animal, for the red deer is wholly lost to Wales, which is a far
larger and wilder area. The truth of the matter, or at least there
seems little reason to doubt it, is that the Exmoor deer owe their
continued existence to the sport of stag-hunting and the virtu-
ally unbroken maintenance of a pack of staghounds on Exmoor
for at least two hundred years.

Through all the ages the red deer have been the big game of
the hunter, possessing a mysterious and almost sacred significance. The lordly stag was the desire of the lynx-eyed hunter
clasping his bronze-headed spear, and the quarry of bearded
king with ringing bridle and golden spurs upon his heels. He
was the beast that gave sport to the feudal nobles and to the
lords and ladies bewigged on high blood-horses. He was the
magnet that drew the horsemen in hundreds to the moors of
Devon and Somerset in August and hot September. He was the
reason, long ago in the dark past, for the Crown laying hold of
the hills for a Forest, because of the desire of kings for his flesh
and the sport of his running. Looking back through the years,
there has never been a time, as far back as memory goes, when
the stag on Exmoor has not been a beast of the chase, and
therefore a venerated and protected beast.

Whether kings themselves, or what kings, ever came to hunt
on Exmoor we do not know, for there are no records of such
things, or at least none surviving, but the old Saxon monarchs
are said to have had a palace at Porlock, maintained no doubt
as a hunting-box. The kings of Wessex certainly hunted in
North Somerset, and the chronicle of Edmund and Dunstan
gives a vivid glimpse of the nature of such sport. If the medieval
kings did not hunt the Exmoor deer themselves, at least it seems
fairly certain, from the proximity of Dunster Castle and its
lordly associations, that princes and nobles did, though again
there are no records. The story of the hunting of the deer is
largely unknown and unrecorded until the middle of the eighteenth century, when the famous old pack known as the North
Devon Staghounds emerges into the light of history under the

patronage and mastership of the Acland family. From then on the annals of stag-hunting and the fortunes of the deer are fully recorded down to the present day. Books, hunting diaries and other papers contain a wealth of information of every sort, and chief among the things they tell us is that there has been no time, despite an apparent break between 1825 and 1852 (when the old pack was sold), when the deer have not been hunted, and that it is to the management and custodianship of the hunt that the deer owe their survival today in a truly wild state. Without this guardianship the wild deer of Exmoor would have ceased to exist long ago, exterminated like their relatives in all other parts, by irate farmers on one hand and rapacious poachers on the other. To the Devon and Somerset staghounds both the deer and the lovers of the deer owe a great debt.

So well have the deer prospered under the auspices of the hunt that they are now gradually increasing in numbers, and have in recent years spread south and west from their stronghold of Exmoor to repopulate the woods and combes of mid Devon even as far as the Cornish border and beyond. May they continue to prosper for their own well being and our delight.

The small dappled calves of the red deer are dropped some time before or around midsummer, but one seldom sees them because it is the habit of the hinds to hide their young ones in the deep bracken until they are old enough and strong enough to keep pace with the adults. One seldom sees deer anyway, except in the early morning or at twilight. Unless disturbed, they are largely creatures of the dawn and the dusk and the moonlight, preferring to couch in the fern or the depth of the wood during the noonday period, from whence they emerge to graze at night. Yet sometimes one does come upon them unawares, and I have seen them today, and remember, once on another summer's morning, descending a small lonely combe about the headwaters of Badgery, with the bracken head-high and the wind towards me, and on stepping down to the crossing-place coming face to face with a hind drinking. I had been masked by the fern to the very last moment, and if she had heard or seen any slight movement she had no doubt associated it with nothing more dangerous than the wandering of a hill sheep. For one brief moment we stared at one another, within touching distance, and then she, golden with summer, wheeled and leapt from the stream and went bounding up the bracken slope. Half way up she stopped again and looked back at me questioningly, her big ears pricked and wide. Then she gave a sudden sharp bark, almost dog-like, and was gone.

Stags are even less likely to be seen at this time of year, for they are 'in the velvet', lying-up miserably in all the discomfort of growing their new horns. The antler grows, as the folk say, 'with the bracken', starting its protuberance in May and reaching its full growth about the end of July, during which time the horn is covered with a membrane or 'velvet' of blood vessels. By August the antler has hardened and the velvet shrivelled, and the big summer stag is ready and fit to hunt, and the red coats will go by in the morning, bright in a world of green, to rouse the lord of the woods to his ancient destiny and start another season on the hills.

§

A GREY morning on the hills, with all the rise and fall of the moor a dark reflection of the low billowing cloud above, and all around the wide expanse of fern-bed surging to meet one like the margin of a green sea breaking at one's feet. The sheep in the bracken raise their heads and start like shying horses as they hear my footsteps, and go bounding down the slope and over the rocks in wild unreasoned panic. Wild white faces, chalk-white and bony like skulls, long rabbit-ears, legs like goats and tails that bob like brushes behind them—Cheviots, the sheep of the Border, far off from their northern home.

They are the sheep of the Forest here, longest established of all the out-country breeds, and bred today on most of the Forest farms. The first of their kind were brought down from the north, I believe, by the Knights, who settled them here on the new-made farms and saw them prosper and flourish. Since then many new breeds of sheep have been introduced to the moor, Blackface and Swaledale, Welsh and Clun, but none— save the Scotch Blackface—have stayed to rival the Cheviot on the rough, high ground.

I walk on over hill and combe, across many small streams and through wind-bleached gates in old boundary walls, picking my way about the uneasy bogs, until at length the land begins to fall away westwards, and the rift of valley drops steeply to heather and the lower ground. Away at the head of the combe rises the Longstone, a dark finger thrusting up from the sullen earth, and beyond it a long skyline crowned with barrows.

Through sedge and nodding cotton-grass and over soggy and uncertain ground I approach the Longstone, glad of my heavy boots. As I come slowly to it, it seems to advance towards me, almost as though to meet me. This is a strange illusion, no doubt common to other standing stones, but I know of no explanation for it. It seems like a tall figure regarding one, a presence, immemorial, brooding and somehow sinister. How eerie it must be in the fog, or at twilight—but I would not like to be up here then, on this boggy and trackless ground.

The sun comes out as I at length reach the stone, and its awesomeness is dispelled, though not its mystery. It stands, a slab of slaty blue-grey rock, some nine or ten feet tall (or so I should guess), flattened and irregular in form with average dimensions of about six or so inches thick and two feet wide. At its foot a smaller slab is set, as a calf to a cow, also on end. One stands now before it and wonders—wonders what hands upreared this monolith in what ages past, and for what purpose. It stands high up, yet not on the top of a hill as do the barrows —on desolate ground facing downwards to the settled land, and its thin edges seem to run north and south. Probably it belongs to the era of Avebury and Stonehenge, and to the days of the Bronze Age people, but beyond this its origin and purpose can only be guessed at. All the questions that come crowding in on one's mind—from what rift or rockfall this was heaved out, what manner of people toiled to drag and erect it up here and with what ceremonies it was hedged about—can never be answered now, and one can only feel towards an explanation. Symbol of a god, monument of a chieftain, place of sacrifice, boundary of a kingdom? No one knows. I only know that there is about it something dark and potent.

There are other standing stones of various sorts on and about the moor, though none so tall and forceful as the Longstone. All of them are equally mysterious. They are usually regarded as markers of the bounds of Forest and parish, but like the barrows that are likewise said to serve this purpose they are mostly immeasurably older than such medieval conceptions—it is more likely that Forest and other bounds were fixed by landmarks that were already there, rather than the reverse. The Caratacus Stone on Winsford hill has an inscription in Latin characters incised upon it, which sets it into the Romano-British period, and so makes it a very late comer into the megalithic company. The inscription, I think, reads CARATACI NEPUS, which would seem to mean that the stone was erected by a kinsman of one Caratacus, but here again, who he was or precisely why the stone was erected is something that cannot be said. The small odd stones that one often comes across set on end on patches of flat open ground have probably been set as sheep-scratchers in recent times, by moor farmers hopeful of keeping sheep off their backs in the season preceding shearing.

After walking on up to the ridge of the hill to look out over the wide view on the far side, I turn and come down by the Longstone. Again I have that feeling that it is advancing to meet me. As I pass and turn my back on it I feel almost as if it were watching me. There is certainly 'something' about it.

Suddenly, as I face the southern skyline, there is a horseman on Longstone Barrow. He sits there motionless, like a dark phantom risen from the earth. Only his horse's tail blows in the wind. He is the perfect figure in this timeless setting—its natural emanation. He does not move as I approach, and then I see he has two dogs, black-and-white collies, at his horse's feet. He is a shepherd and they his sheep-dogs, but he might so easily be an Arthurian prince with his horse and hounds.

I come down slowly from the high places, and retrace my steps by the way that I came this morning. The wild white sheep forage still amidst the bracken and bent, but now there are cattle too, a herd of black beasts spread out over the wide rough moorland pasture. Those nearest to hand raise their black polled heads to look at me as I pass. They are the Forest Galloways, and like the Cheviot sheep are strangers from the north. The first of them were imported some time about 1933 by the Fortescue estate and have since become thoroughly established on all the high moors of the district. They seem to suit well to the conditions of the Forest, and they winter out, the only concession to wintering being that they are brought down closer to the lonely ranch farms for the hardest months.

They look very impressive now, knee-deep in the rough growth, with the long grey skyline beyond. Their coats are very black and fairly smooth now, though in winter time they grow thick and shaggy as bears. The calves that run with them are deep brown, rusty-coloured under the buttocks, a reminder that perhaps dark dun was the original colour of this hardy and ancient northern breed.

The going is deep and heavy as I come down to the heather again upon the common that leads to home. It is the zenith of the year, and all growth is at its fullest. The fern brushes my thighs and the big heather is knee-deep. Already the rich purple of the bell-heather has broken in small patches in sheltered and south-facing places, fore-runner of the Tyrean sea to come, and the delicate pink heath nods in profusion. Along the banks the first whortleberries are ripe under their small crisp leaves. The heavy beech hedges sigh with a sound like the surf on the shore as the evening wind ruffles their leaves, and from the fields comes the sweet heavy perfume of the wild white clover. The golden tangle of honeysuckle falls amongst the branches here and there, and wild roses, cerise-pink, shed petals on the grass. Summer, and all the fullness thereof.

§

ACROSS THE little fields the walls and roofs of the old farm arise from their knot of trees. A long low house built of old grey stone, rough ancient work, turns blank walls to the outer world, and a thick roof of moss-grown thatch comes down low like a brim to meet the stonework. Only one tiny stair-light breaks the long windowless range. From one end of the house a slate-roofed shippon extends, and there are other shippons and a barn on the far side. No sound of life arises from the yard as I come to it but the splashing of water falling on stones and the sudden flutter of a bird.

Again I stand in the old yard on this July morning, and the birds are singing in the trees. The grass grows tall by the stream, for the farm has been deserted and empty these past two years. It has a forgotten dreamlike quality. The yard grown knee-high with tall grass, the little stream running through the middle like a silver ribbon, the old silent house on one side and the barns grass-grown about the threshold on the other—all give a sense of timelessness. A great beech tree stands guardian behind the barn and throws a deep pool of shadow across to the house. On the other side is a tall ash tree. Between them a gate opens to a little rough pasture, all rush and sedge, an antechamber to the moor, and beyond is the moor itself, tawny space pressing in on the green fields like the sea about the shores of an island.

The ancient house seems to sleep under its deep smooth thatch dreaming of who-knows-what. And waiting. Somehow there is a sense of *waiting*. Something seems to be sleeping yet waiting, almost watching, behind those old windows and black oak iron-studded door. The sun pours into the courtyard, filling it as a vessel is filled. There is no sound or movement except for the rippling splat and the blackbird singing in the tree. It is a place that seems for the moment wholly like a dream, like a scene from some old romance.

It is said to be haunted. Previous occupants have described strange happenings from time to time, queer noises at night and the mysterious movement of objects. Older generations ascribed such manifestations to 'pixies', and the present-day one to a poltergeist. But I myself have felt nothing disturbing within the old empty house, only a sense of sadness and loneliness.

It is one of the very ancient farms of Exmoor, one which time has left behind and which holds itself in most ways scarcely changed from oldest farming times. The rough stone walls, buttressed in part against the naked rock of the yard, have never known rendering or whitewash. The thatch that comes low to meet the grey stone is as it has always been. The barns and shippons too were thatched until a short while ago, until the thatch began to fall in and was replaced by tin and some slates. The splat that falls over a stone ledge into the yard has provided water for man and beast for as long as the farm has stood. Within, the house follows the usual pattern of all such dwellings. A kitchen, a back kitchen, a parlour, a dairy behind and a narrow twisting cupboard-stair leading to connecting bedrooms above. There are big hearth fireplaces, stone-flagged floors, small deep windows and old oaken doors set together with handmade nails. Once it must have been all warm and bright, with big fires of wood and peat on the open hearths, and noisy with household bustle, and once the parlour was proud with linenfold panelling (this I am told was torn out a generation ago). Once folk dug peat on the hill for winter fires and faggoted the hedgings, and baked and brewed, and herded sheep and cattle in the yard, and brought home the sheaves of corn from the little fields. Once pack-horses clattered in from the rocky trackway, and men rode out to hunt or herd, and children played by the water-splat.

But such days are gone, and the house waits in loneliness while another farm tills its fields and holds its common rights. Its fate is that of so many others of its kind. Cut off from the world of the automobile by its lack of road, and not large enough by standards of present-day economy to justify the expense of modern improvements, it has no future before it as an independent holding, and so must merge with some other more favoured farm.

Ironically it is the coming of the motor-car that has rendered so many of the old farms more isolated than ever they were in olden times. A generation or so ago all moorland roads were more or less equally good—or more precisely, equally bad—and in consequence all folk and all business went by horseback.

The doctor, the vet, the parson, the postman and all country callers rode from farm to farm about their business, over the muddy tracks and down the stony lanes, and no one place was more lonely or cut off than another. Nowadays all these folk travel by car alone, and as the average car goes only where the tarmac runs, and the tarmac goes only where it is economic for it to go, so has it come to pass that many of the smaller holdings have been forced into an isolation that few folk care to endure.

I turn away through the gate that leads to the moor, and walk up away from the sad and lonely yard through the brushing rushes towards the sky. The tussocky ground is rough and heatherless, for here is the edge of a bog, and underneath is the deep, wet peat. Once the black turf was dug for the hearth of the lonely house below, but no one digs it now, though the hours are long and sunny. Yet now is the season, the long hot sunny days of summer, when the moor folk used once to find time away from other things and go up to the hill to cut peat for their winter fires. Everywhere on the moor one finds the dark, water-filled, rush-grown hollows of the old peat-diggings, black sinister pitfalls for the unwary rider or careless bullock. Nowhere, though, does one see peat cutters at work. In these days if one is not satisfied with wood then it is easier to buy coal than to dig peat. The last peat-ricks or turf-burrows that I ever saw, conical coal-black beehives on the ridge of the high moor, were upon Brendon Common about ten years ago.

The black peat lies everywhere just under the surface of 'spine' or rough moor herbage, but is best and deepest in the region of bogs. I came across a peat-face the other day, freshly broken by the action of the weather and standing as a miniature cliff on the slope of the hill. The first 'spit' was a conglomeration of rough tight-pressed brown herbage, the second spit was true peat, black as coal and quite hard, and below that under a definable iron-pan were clay and shillet, and the rock. The depth of peat varies of course in different places, from a few inches to many feet.

Peat falls, or used to fall, into two classes: spine turf and pit turf. The spine turf was that lying near the surface just under the herbage growth, and largely composed of recent fibre, and was such as could be skimmed off easily, but the pit turf, the real coal-black peat of the high moor, came only from the deep bogs and, as its name implied, was dug from pits or trenches. In places such bogs might be almost bottomless, and the digging would go down for the depth of many spits.

Various tools were used for the cutting of the peat, chief of which was the peculiar-shaped spade with which the clats were cut and prized out. Having cut one's peat one stood two clats up together to dry, and then afterwards carted them straight home to be stored in a shed, or put them up in a rick to be moved later. If one ran into heavy or continuous rain during the proceedings, one's peat was apt to dissolve, I gather, and the result of one's labours to be brought to naught. A sledge would seem to have been used for carting on the rough and soggy ground in the vicinity of the bogs wherein a wheeled vehicle would have stuck, or sunk; and I have, in fact, seen old photographs showing such transport.

The black peat of the moor has given fuel to many generations of hill folk, and would seem also to have given its name to many places in the region. The prefix 'black' is frequently to be met with—as in Blackpits, Blackford, Blackland—and in many cases has obvious meaning, though it should be remembered that the term 'black' also implies heather ground.

Turbary, the right to cut turf on the common, was one of three primary common rights held by farmers and commoners of each moorland parish. In general the common rights, which seem to have existed 'from such time as the memory of man runneth not to the contrary', gave to each holding in the district the right of pasture, to summer-graze on the moor as many sheep, cattle and horses as could be over-wintered in ground, the right of turbary, to dig peat for the hearth fire, and the right to cut bracken and rushes for bedding, etc. Today few people cut fern and no one seems to cut peat, but the pasture rights are still most valuable, and everywhere the hill is heavily stocked with sheep and cattle and a considerable number of ponies.

It is late when I come home, and the moon is in the sky. I am greeted with the news that some of our cows have broken out and are mingling with a herd of moor cattle up on the edge of the bog. So it's up to the moor in the moonlight to try to sort out our beasts and bring them home. Out from the lane we blunder about knee-deep in grass and rushes between the hedge and the fringe of the bog, trying to find the dark forms of cattle, trying to see what is ours and what is black and what is dark red (almost impossible in the moonlight). The beasts are scary and restless in the night, appearing and disappearing between the pools of moonlight and the black swallowing shadows, and the horns of the Devons rise against the moonlit sky like the horns of aurochs in great ritual curves.

In the end we prevail and succeed against all expectations in driving our cows back to their proper domain. We try to mend the broken gate with string as a final act, and then walk home through the brushing grass of the hayfields. A great, full orange-coloured moon hangs in the sky. Home, hot coffee and biscuits, and then to bed at last, tired, and very late.

§

THE SUN shines warm on the bog as I pick my way through the expanse of rush and sedge and spongy moss and over the black, sogging peat. A humid warmth rises from it, coming up into

95

one's face like a breath, heavy with the wet bog smell. The wet ground splashes and squelches at every step, yielding and treacherous. Little broken streams from nowhere run this way and that like twisting silvery ribbons, and in the deeper parts of the bog there are long still pools that catch the sun like fragments of a shattered mirror. Many flies and other flying things make a humming over the moss-beds, and grasshoppers chirrup from hidden places, and occasionally a marsh bird rises up startled from the rushes.

In the hollows under the tussocks of rush and sedge the yellow sphagnum moss coils in wet matted cushions all intergrown with slim grasses and water plants. I put my hand down and am surprised, almost startled, to feel the heat of it, for its warmth is quite tropic. I move on, careful of my footing, and lo, here in the midst of the bog is a carpet of flowers like scattered jewels all entwined and embedded in the matrix of wet sphagnum moss. Delicate pink bog-pimpernel, golden marsh St John's worts, the fragile blue of the ivy-leaf bellflower, sweet-scented, golden-starred spikes of bog-asphodel, turquoise water forget-me-nots, malevolent little sundews, lesser skull-cap, marsh-pennywort, small heath-orchis, and taller, yellow, water butter-cups nodding above them all. How lovely they are in their bogland home, islanded by the glistening water.

Hither and thither brilliant dragonflies flit, lovely creatures with glittering, satanic, green bodies and black, gauzy wings, hunting the hag-line of stunted water-sunken alder and willow beyond the bog. A slight breeze catches at the rushes, ruffling them so that they shine like clusters of silver lances in the sun. A lark sings overhead, high and far away.

I pluck a few spikes of the bog-asphodel for the sweetness of their scent, and then pick my way back out of the bog, carefully walking on the spine, treading on the tussocks and turning the rushes with my foot as I go. Despite the treachery of the bogs, there are very few one cannot walk across if one knows how to walk and where. Though rushes may grow in water, they like their roots firmly anchored, and turned with the sole of the foot they will not let you down. Green sphagnum moss on its own spells danger, for usually it lies over liquid peat, and one always avoids it.

The clouds are gathering as I go home. The sun goes in and

out, and finally withdraws its face altogether behind the bank of cloud that rises from the western hills. I hurry on, mindful of our part-made hay that lies in the five-cornered field. The white-tops under the cloud are ominous, and presage a storm.

So once home it's up to the field to cock up the clover hay, which has been turned today, before it rains again. All hands turn to and hustle up extra forks, while someone throws the harness on the horse to rake. It will be a race against time. The cloud is dark and grey and threatening, and every now and then one feels, or imagines one feels, the touch of fine rain on one's face.

The horse-rake starts to clank to and fro across the field, and the first cocks or pooks rise from the ground. The clover is thick and heavy, and raw and green in parts, but it is better up than on the ground, and anyway it will make-out in the cocks. A stiff sou'west wind is keeping the rain up for the moment, but it does not improve the pooking. We all work steadily, unable to hurry at this particular job. Each pook must be carefully made if it is to keep the rain out. Each must go up like a tapering tower, and every pickful[1] of hay must be laid on flat and dead-centre, and the top must be fitted over like a cap, and, to end, the bottom must be scraped clean all around so that it will suck up as little of the wet as possible—more wet goes into a pook from the bottom than the top very often—and then with luck our pooks will turn the rain for a week or more. In the end, though, as with corn, it is the fine insidious rain and wet mist that do more damage than a sharp downpour. Gradually the lines of the pooks lengthen up the field, but gradually too the light begins to fade and imperceptibly it is getting dark. It looks as if we shall be beaten, not by the rain but by the dark. Still we go on, nerved by the gathering storm to the south-west where the clouds sit on the hills. It is too dark now to see the tines of one's fork, and one works by feel and instinct. On and on, and one feels the end will never come. Then at last a voice says out of the darkness: 'That's the lot', and from out of the darkness figures loom up right and left like ghosts from the forest of pooks. Tired but triumphant we shoulder our picks and head for home. Eleven o'clock at night, or nearly so, but we have beaten both the rain and the darkness.

[1] Pick (pike) = pitchfork.

97

§

THE SUN pours down on the hay from a cloudless sky pale
and hazy with heat, while with swinging picks we throw out the
pooks and spread the hay to the joyful radiance. The whole air
is heavy with the scent of the sweet clover hay, and warmth
rises from the hot ground, and one is enveloped in the breath of
it all. Over the hedge the moor sweeps away to the west in
shimmering glowing light, with lilac-blue hills floating in space
between earth and sky, and all around is the fullness of summer.
One sweats as one works, but is contented.

Along the foot of the lower hedge the splat runs sweet and
cool under the fringes of rush and tall water plants. As one
nears it at the end of a pook-row one may walk away from the
dry rustling hay for a moment and stop and stoop for a drink.
The sweet moorland water is cool and silky to the lips, delightful
and thirst-quenching, not icy or hard. Then back again from
the green hollow to the hot, rustling, heavy-scented pooks. The
hayseed fills one's shoes and gets into one's clothes and down
one's back, and one's eyes get tired of the sight of hay; yet what
a joyous world it is when one straightens up and looks around
at the sun-drenched fields and the moor, and up at the arc of
the sky, and knows the delight of a summer's day.

Over by the top hedge the men have laid the staddle of green
beech for the base of the rick, and are setting the elevator in
proper position. On the grass the bits and pieces of the sweep
are being put together and affixed to the front of the tractor.
As soon as all the pooks are out and the sun has done its work
with the first hay we shall begin our 'carrying'.

Now an engine throbs, and the elevator starts to clank and
rattle and the tractor moves off for its first load. We take up our
respective positions, some to be on the rick, and some to 'put
up', and there's a sorting over of picks so that each man may
have the one that suits him best at his particular job. Here
comes the sweep with its first shuffling load, and our rick is
begun. How different it is now we do not use horses. Not very
long ago we loaded the little wagon-carts and brought them
turn and turn about to the rick and put up by hand. Now the
tractor and sweep do it just as quickly and with only one
person's labour for the locomotion. The elevator too makes a

great difference to the rick building, for whereas in former times we had to strain and juggle to put up as the rick grew to a head, we now receive the hay in an easy fall from above—that is, if we don't make the rick too big for the elevator. But haymaking is still haymaking. Like our ancestors before us we are still dependent on the weather and so rejoice in a fine dry day.

The sweep goes to and fro and our rick takes shape and grows. Higher and higher the good hay rises, and we are getting farther from the ground. We are more than knee-deep in the springy stuff and are half smothered by it as it falls upon us in heedless masses. One forks and heaves to keep pace with the almost ceaseless flow, and one's muscles strain and skin sweats. The heat of the rick is like the breath of an oven. The perspiration runs down my face, and my shirt is sticky and full of the scratching, irritating bits and seeds that fall in a continuous shower down my back. How one begins to look with longing and anticipation towards the hayfield gate at intervals of five or so minutes. At last! The gay dresses of the women flutter in the gateway, the wearers moving slowly under the burden of jugs and baskets.

Someone props a ladder against the rick and we scramble down. Everybody gathers in the pool of shade and we all throw ourselves down upon piles of the sweet-smelling hay, in a half-circle, with the baskets set in the midst. The hay tea is an event, a picnic and a social half-hour; even the dogs are admitted to the circle. Sandwiches, scones and buns, cakes and biscuits of every sort are passed round, together with strong tea hot from jugs and cans, and we laze and feast and talk in luxury and at our ease. How good is rest after heavy work, shade after sweating, drink after thirst, food in plenty to a hungry appetite. Perhaps it is in such things that true pleasure lies, and all our cultivated delights but an illusion. The talk turns from one thing to another, of this haymaking and others remembered, the prospects of the autumn sheep trade, the season's stag-hunting that is just before us, the latest bit of scandal from the village. One gossips and eats and drinks, and feels the warmth and roughness of the hay under one's bare arms, and looks up at the eternity of the sky blue above the dry-green grass, and down again at the hedges heavy with leaf and hemmed with foxgloves. At my side the sweep is quiet in the grass. How beautiful with purpose are the long fingers that slide so effortlessly over the ground. They are like the lances of a phalanx of men-at-arms, tough, polished, tapered ash, each tipped with a shining point of steel.

Now we rise once more and turn to work again. The machinery breaks into spluttering noise, and hot hands reach for the picks. Our rick grows higher still, though perhaps only so very high in our own estimation, for Exmoor ricks are not very big according to general standards—they tend to be long and low, perhaps to escape the wild winds, and small because the fields are small. The hay seems hotter than ever, though perhaps this too is an illusion, and the smell overpowering and almost stifling. Someone has the good thought to throw up a bottle of drink on to the rick. Round and round we work, end, middle, end and round again, forking and treading, with the pick-handles almost bending under the strain—what a delusion it is that hay is a light and airy substance—and ducking all the while under the fangs of the elevator, which when not deluging us with smothering hay threatens our heads as with remorseless iron teeth. Now the area is growing less as we start to head out and the rick grows to an apex. The view is glorious when one has a second to notice it—here are our little fields seen as from a tower, and yonder is the moor bathed in radiance and dotted with grazing flocks and herds and speaking of space. Some of the hay is coming up a trifle green now, and there are rude remarks about 'frying our breakfast on it in the morning', but as it is in the head it will not hurt. The main thing now is to get it up. One never trusts Exmoor weather. Tomorrow it may pour with rain.

The apex of the rick has narrowed now to a yard's width, and there is only room for one. I slither down and feel for the top rung of the ladder and descend to earth again. The man remaining tops up the ridge and then he too descends and the machinery stops for good. The only thing now left to do is to throw up the rick-sheet and spread it over the head.

The last rays of the sun are coming low through the hedge as we go home down the lane, and there, over a swinging gate, we see red cattle where no cattle should be. Some moor cattle have broken in. We give the alarm, and having got reinforcements (two humans and three or four dogs) set out to eject them. The cattle dog flies round them, but they do not drive. Instead they bunch and lower their heads to the dog. They have calves with them and they resent molestation in their new-found paradise of grass. I go after them and they wheel and break away in the wrong direction. Running, we follow them down and turn them, and begin a glorious chase round the field. They are angry now, these great Devon cows usually so placid, and down go the great-jowled heads, and again one hears that strange wild howling roar that seems not the lowing of any domestic beast, but rather the prelude to the charge of a wild thing. The white horns flash like scimitars and they charge at the dog. Like an eel he evades the lunges, and I run in shouting and brandishing my stave. They wheel again, and run this time for the gate, and the dog and I run with them. Huge red bodies plunging through the grass, heads down, lunging and snorting—every nerve seems to leap, and I shout wildly as my feet fly on tireless and the dogs race and bark like harrying furies. So must man once have hunted before ever the milk-pail was or cow stood in a stall.

We are at the gate now. I could almost let them slip back for the joy of the chase again. But they are through and pounding towards the moor, and we harry them up the lane a way for good measure. Now at last dogs and humans calm down and we return to shut the gate. The shafts of light are gone from the lane. The sun has slipped beyond the rim, and our faces are towards home and rest.

August

A FINE morning, with the sun rising for another hot day. The first of August, and today we dip the sheep.

Noise and confusion and shouting and the barking of dogs. Extra hands bringing up the tractor and drum for relays of water, and the man who is to stand at the dip donning a black raincoat and thigh-boots like a man-at-arms preparing for battle. Now the first sheep are in the pens, the dip fresh-filled, yellow and baleful, the man ready in the pit, and self and farmer ready to catch and throw in. So we begin.

One by one the struggling, wild-eyed sheep are seized and by brute force dropped in backwards with great splashes as though over a cliff edge. They fight as only hill sheep can, setting their legs, twisting, plunging, pitting all their weight and sinew and cunning against the catchers. But in they go in the end, as though to their doom, down into the seething bath below. The dipper wrestles with them, three or four at a time, pushing them under and turning them, holding them for the regulation time, until at last they are allowed to find their feet on the steps of the ramp at the other end, and scramble out all dripping into the far pen.

As the catching-pen empties so we drive another batch in, thirty or forty at a time, cramming them like sardines. It is non-stop and hard work. The driving-in is something of a primitive hunt, with dogs and humans all yelling like savages and trying to force a batch off from the spinning, terrified flock and up the wired race to the catching-pen. The speed at which a sheep can move and the cunning and skill with which it can double and twist in a confined space are amazing. A dozen times an old ewe will evade capture, out from between three or four people, and in a last resort charging straight towards one with a force that will flatten one if hit. In the last penful, at the end of a flock, one always gets the worst and most difficult characters —those sheep whose cunning has enabled them to escape from all preceding drives.

All day we work, and the catching-pen becomes a small slippery arena, in which it is difficult to keep one's footing, and many times the dip itself has to be replenished. Gradually we work through the flocks. First the ewes and lambs, Exmoor and Closewool, then the blackfaced Dorsets, and then the hoggs, then lastly and at length the rams. The big fellows come quietly, led on strings like dogs. Save for their big size they are no trouble and offer less resistance to the dip than the ewes. Old Jumbo, the huge Dorset ram, goes in with a splash that nearly drowns everybody, and then sits up like an old gentleman in his bath. His sides stick tightly against the walls of the dip, and there is some question as to whether he is wedged for life. However, he too comes up out of the dip at last, and it is finished. Dipping is over for another year.

Having stood long enough to drain, the sheep go back to

their respective fields, and we wash at the splat and go in to tea.

Our sheep come away from the dip only slightly yellowed and by the time they are dry there will not be any colour on them at all. The days of 'bloom' are past, and no one, or hardly anyone, uses a bloom dip any more. Once it was the fashion in these parts to mix a strong yellow-ochre dye with the dip so that the sheep came out golden like mythical beasts and carried the colour through the time of the autumn sheep sales. Certainly this old practice gave the sheep a lovely look, and I remember the glowing flocks coming down to Exford auction like a picture, and the tethered rams that wanted but the gilding of their mighty horns to make them each the Golden Fleece of some far-roving Jason. The wool merchants, however, now discourage the use of bloom on the grounds that it damages or discolours the wool, and so it is only a very few conservative farmers who continue to use it.

§

HEATHER IN August. Here I sit with the heather all about me, purple, glorious, spread like a cloak over the moor. All around it swirls and tosses in the racing silky wind, lilac and amethyst and Tyrean crimson, like a coloured, foaming sea, bewildering the senses with the ceaseless whirling movement. The honey-sweet scent of it, wonderful, wine-like, warm in the sun, blown in one's face by the west wind, is intoxicating, and an elixir to body and spirit alike. I stretch half sitting, half lying, and looking up see the host of exquisite amethyst sprays tossing against the blue of the sky like a revelation in light and colour. For one transcendent moment the colour is a voice and the moment all eternity.

Bees drowse over the heather, themselves seeming half intoxicated by the honey of the purple bells, and innumerable brown butterflies rise and fall and pause to stretch their wings upon the flower-heads. Grasshoppers sing unseen beside me, and overhead a buzzard banks lazily as it quarters the moor from the sky. Oh, the heather, the dear purple heather! If freedom had a flower for its emblem it would be the heather, the purple flower that blows in the sea wind on the wild open hills, free and unconfined, content with the harsh mountainside, sweet in the sun, untrammelled and lordly in fierce independence, defiant before the face of the storm, conferring all of its own deep spirit on those who tread its measureless spaces.

Exmoor heather is composed of three different species, each of which may produce several different colour varieties. Firstly —for it is the first of the heathers to flower in the summer sun— comes *Erica tetralix*. This, the cross-leaved, or rose-pink, heath, begins to open its bells about midsummer. It is a plant more tolerant of wet ground than the others of its kind, and is generally prevalent round about boggy parts. It is also the first heather to recover after the process of swaling, and its pink heads nod gaily over the open spaces before its other relatives have revived their strength. Its normal colour is a lovely graduated rose-pink, but it may vary from a most delicate shell-pink to a rich cerise. A white form is not uncommon, and on one occasion, high on the Forest, I came across a whole patch, possibly an acre in extent, of these pure white bells. It was a magical sight.

The next in order of flowering is *Erica cineria*, the purple bell-heather. This too begins to open its bells soon after midsummer, but does not enter into its full glory until August. Then what a blaze it makes! Its crimson-purple is the royal colour of an emperor's coronation robe thrown out across the moor. It seems to have a preference for dry ground, and is at its finest on a raised bank or any fairly well-drained position. There is a white variety of *Erica cineria*, but it is not at all common, and I have only seen it once myself. Rarest of all, and most beautiful, is the carmine-red variety. I have had the good fortune to come across this two or three times, and in every case the pure carmine bells were longer and narrower—that is to say less globular—than the common sort, and quite distinctive. I also once saw a little bush that was rose-pink.

Lastly, flowering at its best about mid August, or perhaps later, comes *Culluna vulgaris*, the so-called common or Scotch heather. This seems to be a heather of wide adaptability, for it grows on both dry thin ground and on comparatively damp ground where bits of it intermingle with coarse grassy growth. Its general colour is a lovely lilac-purple, softer than the purple of the flaring bell-heather, but it is subject to many subtle gradations—pale lilac, amethyst, mauve-pink and occasionally rose. It is the pure white variety of this species—*Culluna vulgaris alba*, I think it is called—that is the traditional white heather of good luck. Here and there on remote stretches of moorland one can still find a little bush of Exmoor white heather, set like a fairy amongst its purple brethren. Unfortunately it stands little chance of survival should it thoughtlessly grow in parts frequented by human beings for, alas, as soon as its flowers show it is torn up by greedy passers-by.

All three species of heather may grow together on one patch of ground, intermingled in lilac and purple splendour, or they may be locally distinct, one area of moor carrying only one sort and another part growing a different sort. All are generally at their finest in mid August, though the *Culluna* does tend to be a little later than the other two. Incidentally I do not use the term 'ling' because, though in most parts it is taken to mean the common heather, I have heard it used here to denote its opposite, the bell-heather. The scent of all three species is exquisite, but the strongest and sweetest of all, I think, is that of the bell-heather, *Erica cineria*. It is as warm sweet honey in the sun.

Over the heather the many brown butterflies shimmer, and amongst them one small blue one like a chip of sky fallen to earth. Most of the butterflies of the moor seem to be fritillaries of one sort or another, generally small, though occasionally one may have the good fortune to see a finer insect. Once I came upon a great Silver-Washed Fritillary sunning itself in a sheltered spot, its glorious fire-bronze wings outspread in a splendour of at least three inches. Once, too, I saw a Painted Lady on the flowering heather, lovely in the sun.

As I come down from the moor, a bunch of heather in my hand, I pass by a goyal cleft in the hill. A blaze of scarlet strikes my eye, the vivid red of rowan berries, blood-coloured fruit of the twisted trees that are rooted in the rocks. I stop to marvel at them and to break one heavy brilliant spray to put with the purple of my heather. Here is the mountain ash in its true setting, bold and independent like the heather, defiant of wind and weather, proud in its struggle for sustenance amongst the rock and acid peat. How sad and homesick must be those poor trees, trimmed and pruned, their silver trunks all smutty, that live their lives in exile in small suburban gardens, planted there for the sake of their bright berries in the late summer months.

I linger for a while by a sunny bank, for here the whortleberries are ripe and sweet and plentiful. It is pleasant to gather the small, round, blue-black, delicious fruits into the palm of one's hand and pass them into one's mouth, but I would not undertake to pick a basketful for wealth untold. The strain on one's patience—on mine at least—is far too great. One fumbles under the leaves, collecting and dropping the small things, inevitably losing half the spoils in the transference to the container, and equally inevitably dropping or upsetting the container at the precise point where one has begun to think that some progress in filling has at last been reached. Delicious though whortleberry tart, jam and jelly may be, I feel that its cost in terms of nervous strain is too great, and so choose to forgo it unless someone else does the picking.

The lane that leads away from the moor holds easier pickings. Here on both sides of the road, tall and thick, the wild raspberries grow. Their canes are loaded now with the sweet-flavoured red fruits, and unlike the whorts these are simple and easy to pick. Many pounds of jam one can make from a single picking if one knows the right route to take. The wild raspberry is native to the country hereabouts, and in many places—at least along the southern edge of the moor—is more prolific than the bramble.

Nature is lavish now. Whortleberries and raspberries in plenty, blackberries already ripening, rowan and elder if you care to make jelly, and the first delicate-flavoured pink mushrooms in the grass. There is much to be had of the country if you know where to look, and a garden will render you back a hundredfold now—'The earth and the fulness thereof.'

As I come home tonight there is a clopping of hoofs in the lane behind me. I step aside to let the horseman pass, half turning to see the rider. It is the harbourer going out to harbour the stag for tomorrow's meet. His field-glasses swing from his shoulder, the heavy raincoat is strapped before him, and he sits his strong pony with the ease of a man whose life is spent in the saddle. While we are thinking of bed tonight he will be about the dusky woods and places haunted by the deer, and he will sleep—if he sleeps at all—at some lonely farm and be up at the first glimmer of dawn to read the slots and signs of the deer as a lesser man will read a book. He is the man who can tell the age and sex and size of a deer, and the time of its passing, from the slots of its feet in the soft, damp ground, who knows more of the ways of the gold-brown beasts than any man in the land; and he it is who will lead the hounds to where the big stag lies in the maze of the woods tomorrow. His skill and his office are unchanged from the Dark Ages and he lives as few men live today, his world the world of beasts and dawns and dusks, and wet woods in the rain. Some day I will try to paint a picture of him, as I have so often seen him, riding out across the moor, with the sunset in the pools between the rushes, and himself a figure dark against the glowing skyline.

§

AUCTION morning. The heavy transport vehicles come bumping down in an almost ceaseless stream into the low riverside field that is the auction yard, lurching and jerking and ploughing into the muddy ground as they find their way along the long lines of hurdled sheep-pens that stretch across the still green grass. Big cattle lorries like unwieldy juggernauts that seem as though they might tip over at any moment from their own top-heaviness, big high-railed trailers towed by spluttering tractors, boxes and small trailers towed by Land-rovers, trucks with nets over their backs, and all the lot crammed full with fearful bewildered sheep. Auction morning, the first of the autumn sheep sales, and here are our sheep coming into the pens and under the hammer, the end-product of all our labours and the main harvest of our year.

One by one the transports disgorge their bleating cargoes, and one after another the drafts of sheep are driven into the numbered pens. A few small flocks arrive on the hoof—but not many. For the days are past when the flocks from the hills all came down, close-herded by men on horseback, and guarded by the lean, half-bred collies with suspicious eyes. Men are hurrying everywhere, tan-faced farmers in raincoats, gumbooted and

wearing waterproof leggings, striding over the hurdles and seeing their sheep are settled aright, strengthening the pens here
and there with a ramming-iron and exchanging comments
with each other. Down by the entry-way the traffic is getting
worse, for now many of the lorries are turned around and
trying to get out, meeting the incoming transports head on in
the narrow approach. The policeman at the gate has his work
cut out today. Meanwhile, the edges of morning sunshine come
and go, and sudden squalls of rain sweep intermittently across
the field, turning the trodden ground to running mud along the
way and making the folk turn their collars up.

I walk slowly along the lines of pens, looking down upon the
sheep in their thousands. Ewes, hoggs, lambs and rams. The
Exmoor Horns predominate, and after them the Closewools,
then come sundry other breeds. Wild-eyed Scottish Blackface,
hawk-faced Cheviots and Border Leicester crosses, plump
Downs Blackface—mostly Dorsets—and some Cluns and a few
odd sorts to finish with. Most of the pens have the names of the
owner-breeders pinned up in pride as well as the common
place-numbers, and everyone is interested in other folks' stock.
There are prizes, too, today, for the best ram and the best pen
of lambs, etc., and there's an air of a show as well as a sale
about the morning's fixture.

Now the auctioneer's rostrum is out and heading for the first
line of pens. A wonderful affair it is—an old farm wagon with a
roof affixed above, and a desk along the off-side, and the horse
that draws it is truly a sight to behold in this commonplace
world. The noble beast is resplendent in polished harness
plated and decked all over with flashing brasses and trimmed
with ribbons, and he moves with ponderous and stately tread
as though he knew the great responsibility of his position. The
crowd presses round the wagon as it comes to a halt, and dealers
and farmers jostle to the front. No one seems inclined to stop
talking, so I press forward to hear the first bidding.

'Gentlemen, gentlemen—here's a pen of Horn ewe lambs
from under Dunkery. What shall I put them up at? put them
up at five pounds . . . five pounds I hear—make it guineas . . .
five-one . . . five-two, I hear . . . five-three . . . five-four . . .
five-five . . . five-six . . . five-seven . . . five-seven . . . five-eight
. . . five-nine . . . five-nine . . . five-nine I'm bid. Come along

gentlemen, here's as fine a trip of lambs as you'll find in the country—make it five-ten . . . five-ten, going at five-pound-ten a piece—gone to Mr——' The hammer drops. The horse takes a pace forward. 'A pen of wether lambs straight off Withypool Hill—who'll bid me . . . ' So it goes on. Our auctioneer knows all his customers, sellers and buyers alike, by name and by reputation, and jokes are cracked along with the more serious business in hand, and the day goes cheerfully despite the showers.

Presently I move away and down the yard to the wide-open door of the large storage shed that does duty as a tea-and-snack bar on such occasions. Hot tea and buns are very welcome on a raw morning, and the concern is doing a roaring trade. Temporal needs satisfied, I leave the auction and the village and walk away up the hill towards the moors. The sun is shining now and the clouds are falling away, and the heather hills rise purple and beckoning towards the sky.

Somewhere over the hill the hounds are hunting, for the season's stag-hunting began two weeks ago, and a Thursday is always one of their days. Perhaps I shall see something of them before I get home—so with ears and eyes alert I step briskly forward into the afternoon sun.

§

I stand in the middle of the circle of stones, and the stones spread all around in a ring, blue in the heather, with the whispering wind about them. Edges of sunlight catch at them, flicker over them and run on down to the combes and distant hills beyond, and the breeze licks at them and at all the heath within and without the circle, and the rushes in the hollow below. Turn your face from east to west and follow the sun, for it is ill luck to turn against the sun in a magic circle!

Some forty stones there are, still standing, and many more lie down or have gone away for ever. The stones that stand are maybe a foot in height, some less, some a little more, all of them worn and weathered by the centuries, chipped and frayed to shadows of what they perhaps once were. The circle itself is some thirty paces in diameter. The ground underfoot slopes a little, opening to the west; and all around is the emptiness of the moor.

My circle is one of several on the moor, all of them small in comparison with the larger and more impressive stone rings in other parts, but round, mysterious and strangely exciting for all that. What hands hewed these stones from some pit or outcrop and dragged them here to stand in a mystic ring? Why are they here in the midst of space? What magical rites were celebrated, what strange gods worshipped here betwixt earth and sky in a ring of stones? There is little to know except that the rings were raised by the Bronze Age men, to keep company with the round barrows on the hilltops, and with the lonely longstones. All the rest is conjecture. That they were connected with the worship of the sun is the most likely guess. Perhaps at the solstices of the year, or at some season of asking, priests and people came up here to the heights to worship and to make offerings, and to seek for a sign.

Look back across the centuries and through the haze of time —perhaps you will see a people dependent on their flocks and herds and little patches of corn, dependent for their survival on sun and rain and the weather of the seasons. On the gods of earth and sun their lives hang, and in them have being, and to such must be made all petitions and observances. Rites, sacrifices, askings. Maybe you will see a procession ascending the hills—people in skins and hides and gaily dyed cloths, warriors on small mealy-nosed horses, a great chieftain in a chariot, priests with ornaments of gold, sacrificial beasts with decorated horns. Who knows?

What was the world when the ring of stones looked in and out upon its makers? Was Troy plundered and burnt, and golden Mycenae above the nations? Was David king over Israel? Had Akhnaton fallen with his divine heresy in Egypt of the Nile? Perhaps. But the hill folk would know little of the mighty things of the stream of life. Theirs was a lesser yet a wilder world. And a wild world indeed it must have been that they looked on —a land rising to the clouds, hill beyond hill rolling and heaving like the sea, golden with sedge or dark with heather, perhaps carrying on its shoulders more scrub than we see today—for scientists tell us that the land was drier then—gouged by goyals and deep valleys matted with woods and choked with oak and rowan and threaded only by the hurrying streams. Below, lapping all around, girding the hills like a great green blanket, would be the primeval forest, broken only by swamp and marsh and tidal river, reaching away in impenetrable sovereignty to where the greater tors of Dartmoor thrust up on the southern horizon. Fearful must have been the winter land, lashed by gales, wrapped in mist, or seared by thunder and lightning, peopled by spirits and dark gods and nameless powers that walked abroad while the wolves howled in the night. Yet beautiful, too, in the summer sunshine, the sky a soaring space above, with the clear air full of the scent of the opening heather and all the herbage a plentiful pasturing for flock and herd, and fat deer in the brake for the taking.

Presently I come down to a stream winding amongst rocks and boulders, and tumbling its way from one ledge to another as it hurries to descend the valley to the larger river below. By one eddy where the water is smoother a heron stands leisurely fishing like a figure on a Chinese vase, and he only bestirs himself to rise in lazy flight at the very last moment of my approach. A little farther on I come suddenly on a small bright pool where the stream falls into a basin of rock under stunted oak and bracken. There is a wild disturbance and about twenty mallard rise from the pool with great whirring and clapping of wings, their brownish bodies wheeling up in great confusion. A lovely sight, and an uncommon one, for wild duck are not usually plentiful on Exmoor.

Down by the bigger river I sit for a while and rest. There is a ripple of movement along the track nearby and a flock of golden sheep, golden like creatures out of some legend or folk tale, comes threading along the moorland road. Their fleeces are soft rich ochre colour, like the gold of the grass on the hills, and they bear on their flanks a bright red cipher like a badge from the age of heraldry. They move on through the bracken, urged by some instinct to a distant place, and presently they are gone. Somebody somewhere must still use a bloom dip in these parts.

I watch the water for a while, until the endless movement of the river and its singing seem to have a mesmeric influence on me, making me feel that I too am being drawn into the flood of movement and carried onwards with its flow. Then I rouse myself and go.

§

Clouds gather now in the hot stillness. Everything is very still and silent with no movement, and no breath of wind stirs anywhere. The atmosphere is oppressive and the sky overhead is turned now to a heavy dark lead-grey, curdled through with an unnatural livid pinkish-brown. Neither bird nor beast calls nor seems to have life.

Now ominous rumbles and mutters of thunder, distant at first, but steadily coming nearer. A few big splattering drops of rain on the dusty dry ground, and suddenly the heavy cloud dissolves into a curtain of torrential rain, coming straight down, loosed like a judgment on the earth. The rain falls with the hardness of hail and a tropical force, pouring on the roofs of house and barn and shippon with deafening noise, pouring in arching jets from every gutter and spout, flooding the yards, turning the splat into a coffee-coloured demon, tearing out the roadway. All the while the thunder comes nearer and louder, its voice above the noise of the downpour like the shouting of a giant. Lightning flickers and shimmers with wicked brilliance on the deluged world. The storm is right overhead now, with terrific crashes and lurid light.

Forked lightning strikes on the moor, and the boiling springs rip strips of earth's flesh from the hillsides and fling it seething into the rivers below. The river itself is a yellow flood, rolling to the bridges with a wrack of torn brushwood and the bodies of sheep trapped on some isle of land. Hay is washed down the fields, and the phone wires are broken and gone and the corn is battered and flattened. All beasts cower from the storm. Two of our red bullocks take shelter in the old open linhay. A flickering viper's tongue of blue light follows them in, and they roll over side by side, never knowing the thing that killed them.

For two hours the storm rages. Then, as suddenly as it began, it ceases and departs. The rain stops. The rags of breaking cloud show wisps of light blue sky, and the air seems cool and fresh

113

again. We look around our soaking world and inspect our damage. Two bullocks struck dead, the phone gone, the roadway surface of the lane torn up in half a dozen places, and banks of shale and debris choking all sorts of awkward places. Our corn is down in patches, but it may rise again—oats will go down three times and come up twice, or so they say. It could have been worse. We shall no doubt hear grievous tales from our neighbours when communications are restored.

Summer storms are sudden and violent, and usually come, as they do in most parts, at the end of a period of hot, dry weather. Heavy heat cloud gathers and breaks upon the hills, and cloudburst sends sheets of water rolling off the barren heights to deluge all the combes and goyals and narrow valleys, and turn the rivers into raging yellow devils tearing out their beds and disembowelling themselves in their fury. All things give way before the flood when it comes and even the bridges may go down in the boiling spate of the waters. In the great flood of 1952, when a huge cloud broke and burst on the roof of the Forest, a dozen or so good bridges were swept down and away by the rivers gone mad in the storm. Mercifully, storms of such magnitude are rare, and no one remembers such a one as that in any long lifetime, or in all the recorded history of the district. Yet storms and floods and storms again there have been, of equal or greater violence, in many ages past and forgotten; for everywhere in every valley where the swift rivers run and meet, the flayed and gaping rocks like riven castles bear mute witness to the raging elements, and testimony to the fury of many waters.

If we are spared the disaster of 1952 in most of our lives, at least we seldom escape the vengeance of the storm gods in some way or other in the course of an average year. Sooner or later thunder rocks the skies and more rain comes down than the earth can hold. Then the streams come up, and not only the streams, but old and forgotten springs hidden away in places unthought of. Now does some malicious genie guide the overflow from the spring-heads down into backyards and into fuel sheds, under the house walls and up through the store-cupboards, up through living-room floors in a swilling mess, on into sitting-rooms, soaking the carpets, and down the doorsteps to earth again. What a mess is water when and where you don't want it, what a precious thing in a drought when you have none and the springs run dry.

For one thing at least we must be thankful: the waters, swift to rise, soon go down again. In a few hours boiling streams and flooded combes empty themselves upon the less fortunate lower regions, and we, though we may have borne the brunt of the storm, are spared the long misery of waterlogged fields and splashing roads that the lowland holdings must endure.

September

THE MOOR is half veiled in mist, wet and sombre, yet flushed under the drizzle with the rose of the heather, as we set out to shift the cattle. As fate has it today we have no horses—only the dogs and our own feet—and the cattle are in a bad temper to start with, and the rain as miserable as can be for the job, for one moves clumsily in heavy boots and a raincoat in summertime.

We reach the end of the lane in fair order, but now the moor opens wide and rolling before the cattle, and they begin to snort and run, and despite all our desperate efforts to hold them in under the hedge they throw up their heads and tails and wheel away into the fenceless space. With the aid of the dogs we manage to head them, and they turn; running hard we manage to get round them, but floundering in Wellington boots over the heavy wet ground, and hot and sweating in streams in the stifling raincoats, we cannot manœuvre quickly enough. Straight for the bog they head now, and into it. We follow them desperately and soon we are all floundering together.

Drifts of rushes waist deep, tall tussocks of sedge, squelching mats of sphagnum moss floating over pools of liquid peat, trails of strange water plants in holes of black water, an insubstantial earth that sways under one's feet, splashing and sponge-like, and yonder a jungle-like thicket of alder and sallow. Here is a realm of another age, one that belongs with bush and swamp and the land of ancient Britain. The floundering red bodies of the cattle heighten the feeling of the primeval, touching some atavistic chord, as though they were buffalo in the swamps of a distant time or place. We stumble and splash, up to our knees in wet peat mire, falling over the tussocks of rank growth, our gum-boots full of thick black water. The cattle buck their way through with mighty squelching. Twice the biggest red beast goes down to her chin, belly-wallowing in black slime, and we think she is bogged good and proper, but twice she heaves herself out with arched spine and legs that fight from the holding squelch with grim sucking noises.

At last we are round them, and at last we are heading for the shore of sound ground where the heather grows. Now we are back to the heath and the gorse, men and beasts together, our feet on *terra firma* once more. The cattle, exhausted by their passage through the bog, are much chastened, and now consent to go the bidden way without further demur.

How dangerous is an Exmoor bog? It is hard to say. Bogs vary in extent and in character, and probably in depth as well. Also they are understandably worse in wet periods than in dry ones. Both sheep and cattle have been known to come to unpleasant ends in the black depths of the various bogs, and there are legends of even horses and their riders being engulfed and swallowed, but I do not know of any authenticated instances of the latter happenings. Certainly the bogs do constitute a great hazard to riders on the moor, but the degree of danger is probably not often much worse than that of a splashing fall. Nevertheless it is wise to treat all bogs with as great a respect as possible and to avoid any approach when on horseback. As to the traveller on foot, I myself have never met any bog that I could not walk across in gumboots, treading upon the spine, but I would not recommend such passaging to any person inexperienced in the ways of the moor. It is much safer and easier to go round, even if it does mean a fairly lengthy detour.

It is a peculiarity of the hill-country bogs that they always occur on high ground. The higher the hill the worse the bog, is the general rule. The biggest and most notable area of bog is the dreaded Chains, high on the roof of the Forest. West Pinford is also a region especially avoided by horsemen, and Ackmead is another. But almost all of the Forest is treacherous in part, and there are few hills that do not carry bog at some place or another in any district of the moor. One just has to watch out for it. So often one may be tempted to ride into bog on seeing hounds and fox flying fleet-footed across it, forgetting that with their greater speed and lighter weight they can skim the spine where a heavier creature will founder and sink.

Another characteristic of the bogs is the general absence of heather upon the surface. Heather does not grow well on wet ground and ceases altogether in truly boggy terrain. Sphagnum moss, sedge, cotton-grass and rush are the chief dwellers thereon, though even rush does not care much for the worst places. Where a thick mat of heather grows there is sound ground, and the same is true of bracken and gorse.

The afternoon begins to clear up a little and the mist to disperse, so that one can see the hills, and even a ray of thin sunshine breaks through. Presently I pass through a neighbour's field where there are more cattle, a big herd of red Devons. A splendid sight they are, with their massive bodies and sweeping white horns, and most splendid of all is the great dark bull who stands in their midst. He stands on a slight rise, and as I walk through the herd I look up to him in passing and see him against the sky. I call out to him—for we are old acquaintances—and he raises his mighty head to look at me for a moment. What a sight he is! At seven years old he is in the prime of his life. His head is so deep-jowled that it is like the head of a monster, his face is covered with the rich dark curls of an Assyrian king, and his horns sweep down and about his red face in two great curving arcs. His neck rises above his shoulders in a bison-like hump, almost black, and all the rest of him is body, mighty and ponderous. So he stands, the mountain of his shoulders dark against the sky, all power and majesty above his herd.

In contrast to cows and steers, whose horns almost always spread out and upwards, the horns of a Devon bull always curve downwards. In a young beast, whose horns are short, this is not noticeable; but in an old one the full-grown horns may often be seen to form a curve right about the face. Drop horns, as these are called, are not, however, entirely the prerogative of a bull, as cows do sometimes throw them, though this is not usual.

The bright interlude of the day seems past. The half-hearted sun has gone again and the clouds are gathered. Behind me the moor has sunk to a wonderful harmony of colours, deep and impressive like a great symphony, with the sky all massive, blue-grey cloud, and the moor sweeping under it in great sheets of dull purple, dusky green, tawny faded gold and wet browns. It rolls dark yet glowing under the now dark sky like mighty music, touching strange depths, and stirring the smouldering passions that sleep under the surface. The presence of the moor is ever with one.

§

THE HOT September sun pours into the harvest field. The rattle of the binder follows the throbbing tractor round the field as, swath by swath, our stand of golden, froth-headed, shining-necked oats diminishes and falls as fat yellow sheaves to the stubbled ground.

Our moorland harvest. The band of helpers moves up and down by the lines of sheaves, raising and stooking them six sheaves to a stook, setting the stooks in rows like heraldry across the field. It is our first task to get the corn up off the ground. Again I lift the sheaves in my arms, the full rustling sheaves, and lifting them see the cascades of pale foaming gold raised against the deep azure blue of the sky. Corn in the sun—ancient and immemorial task, symbol of fulfilment, the promise of food and life. Even in this day the harvest sheaf is sacramental, come to us through generations of hunger and fullness and striving. The heavy tractor is but the logical successor of the sweating horses, and of the scythe and sickle that went before. The sheaf is still the sheaf of Canaan and Egypt.

The sun is hot and the corn dead ripe. The binder is nearing the end of its ruthless course, and soon all the sheaves will be up and stooked. So now we start to make our windmows, beginning across the top of the field. The first, close-packed clump of sheaves is set together, some forty sheaves or thereabouts, heads and butts pressed firmly in well upright; and then another ring is set upon them, and another above this. The windmow mounts up like a golden tower, each course of sheaves covering with its butts the heads of those below, until the conical edifice is some seven, eight or perhaps nine feet tall, with all the sheaf-heads—save those at the pinnacle—safely buried within. A short ladder is called into play for the tying of the top, and the capping of it with an inverted sheaf. Thus we save our corn, or try to, in this country where one never trusts the weather. The Exmoor windmow serves a double purpose: firstly that of securing the corn against the rain, and secondly that of protecting it from the crows. A windmow well and properly made will keep out the rain like a small thatched rick, yet is small enough to allow the corn gradually to dry out and cool within. Usually the sheaves have to stand in the stooks for two or three days to sweat and lose their first heat before being put into windmows, but today our oats are so ripe that they seem fit enough to go up at once. One never takes a chance with the weather if one can possibly help it, for the rain comes all too soon at most harvest times. Our greatest enemy is the wet rain-mist that comes soft and warm from the sea and the hills, and sets the grain sprouting in the head like green grass.

We work on, and the afternoon sun gets hotter as the towers rise about the field. The binder and tractor have finished their work and are drawn into the shade. Somebody calls 'Tea' and we all leave our respective tasks and troop to a windmow near the gate, in the shadow of which an array of tins and baskets has miraculously appeared. We sprawl on the ground under the hedge, and revel in sandwiches and chocolate cake and hot tea out of a can. The dogs are conspicuous by their absence—they are forbidden the harvest field on the cutting day for fear of the binder—but the flies are nuisance enough. Exmoor seems to produce more than the average species of fly—most of which are apt to sting with great vigour.

One looks around as one eats, and has time to think. I remember when instead of the tractor we had three big horses in the binder, dark with sweat and straining in the sun. I remember last year's harvest, when we had corn on the top fields out by the moor, and how the scent of the heather came blowing over the hedge to mingle with the hot grain smell of the oats, and how we carted the corn home in a procession, with the big tractor-trailer leading, and the horses and two little wagons following with their bouncing loads. I remember other harvests when it rained day after day—bitter days of rain—and we watched our corn soaking and sprouting, unable to wind-mow it from the first, and helpless to save it. There is no sadder sight than sodden corn.

Not many farms grow corn nowadays. The climate is all against it, and one needs ready hand-labour to snatch at it between the rains. Once of course a fair amount was grown in the hills—it had to be for the sake of survival—small fields of wheat and barley as well as oats, for home consumption as food for man and beast, and in earlier times rye was no doubt a predominant grain, though of this no memory now remains. Oats still are a good crop here in a good year, but, alas, our harvest months are so very rarely good ones.

We rise refreshed and go back to our labours. Still we stoop to the corn and raise it up to sun and sky and tread the stubble underfoot. We are the votaries of Ceres, busy with a sacred rite. The work cannot be hurried, for the windmows must be well and carefully made, else they will not shed the rain. How long they will have to stand in the field we do not know. A week only perhaps, or perhaps six weeks or even three months. Only the weather knows. I remember once we did not cart until November, and the very last load we brought in on the first weekday of December.

On and on we work till the sun sinks and the twilight creeps around and the moon rises in the east. A great full moon, casting long shadows from the beech hedge, the harvest moon by whose light we still lift the sheaves. Now the afterglow of the sunset reaches out to meet the moonrise and all the land is bathed in a double radiance, magic and mysterious under a velvet sky. There is no time any more, only corn in the moonlight and the immemorial hills.

§

EARLY September, and hotter than August. Already at half past nine in the morning the sun is hot on one's neck and there is a haze of heat over the land turning the hills to blue and silver.

I stand at the top of the wood in the shade, and watch the hounds go drawing gaily down the brake. They push their way through the thick green bracken, and under the branches heavy with leaf, and one can just see their sterns above and amongst the lush and heady tangle. On a lower path a red coat rides, brilliant and vivid in the greenwood, matching the red of the rowan berries as the wearer pushes to and fro. The voice comes up through the veil of leaves, cheerfully calling the hounds to try, and sending them farther down. Foxhounds in the summer sunshine—something little imagined and seldom seen, except in a wild hill country where one must come to terms with the foxes as soon as ever one can.

Beside me, along by the hedge, a group of watchers wait, like myself eager to see the first of the season's sport. The gay summer dresses of the women and the white shirts of the men are far removed from the traditional hunting picture. One feels that either man or Nature has forgotten the seasons, and is confused as to where summer ends and winter begins, and so has put them both together in one piece. Yet this is not the first meet by any means, for hounds have been out since the middle of August, or soon after, cubbing and generally shaking up the foxes, and settling down for the long season to come. Here on the high moor foxhounds hunt a longer season than perhaps anywhere else, for beginning in August they carry on right through into April and sometimes to May, stopped only occasionally by the very worst weather. They are a fine pack, these Exmoor Foxhounds—successors to the old 'Stars of the West'—and work hard for their sport and to keep the wily hill foxes well in hand.

We wait and watch and listen, but no exciting whimper comes up from the growth below, and all there is to hear is the huntsman's voice and an occasional note of the horn. The wood does not hold today and presently huntsman and whip bring the hounds back up and take them on to the steep brake, under the moor. A dozen or so horsemen appear from the side of the wood and go with them, and I follow them down the lane. Not very fast, however, for the lane just here is thick with brambles, and the ripe and shining blackberries are too good to pass unheeded. I fill my hands with the lush juicy berries until the crimson juice runs down between my fingers, and then consume them at my leisure as I go onwards in the wake of the hounds.

Out on the moor the hounds are just swinging down out of sight towards the brake, and the red coats are more vivid than ever as they cross the purple expanse of heather. The master, upon a grey horse, white in the sun, gives a painted brilliance to the scene of colour.

I wait under the hedge that bounds the fields of a farm where foxes are known to run, and sure enough there's the cry of the hounds away below, and coming up towards me—nearer and higher—and then they check, and their voices die away to silence. Scent is bad—it must be on a day like this—and they are at fault in the maze of little fields on the face of the hill. A sudden slight rustle, and out from the beech leaves right before me pops Reynard, down into the heather and away with a bob of his brush that is nearly as big as the rest of himself. I holloa, and so does a neighbour near me. A few more minutes of waiting, and up comes the lifted pack, casting out over the heath. A moment of hesitation, and they then own the line, and away they go over the top of the moor, over and away to the farther valley and combes. I watch them till they are out of sight, and then resume my walk in another direction.

The going is rough and heavy and hot across the side of the common because of the depth of the heather and the thick dwarf gorse that mingles with it. The expanse around me now is a cloak of mingled gold and purple, a brilliant embroidery over the face of the moor. It flowers with the heather, this autumn gorse, in sheets of yellow, while its commoner relative of the spring is sunk into bushes of silent green. *Ulex gallii*, the western gorse, I think it is called, and it creeps low to the ground, six to twelve inches high, seldom more—an undergrowth of lovely flower but bitter scratching spines. It is hard on the feet and noses of beasts, especially dogs and hounds, and only the heavy grazing of cattle seems to hold it in check. It recovers very quickly after swaling, usually ousting other resurgent growth, and seems generally to be on the increase.

After a while the ground becomes easier for walking, and I can look around at things other than my feet. I raise my eyes, and see upon a high and distant ridge a solitary horseman waiting sentinel-like, a watcher on the skyline, like a centaur looking down on the world of men. The solitary horseman in the landscape. He is the epitome of the moor in all its ages.

§

Across the rift of the valley, on the rising ground beyond, almost upon the rim of the hill, the Forest farm is set in its windbreak of toughened trees. Stern and harsh, grey and almost grim, it has the aspect—like so many others of its kind—of a fortress planted here to dominate and hold in subjugation the wild land that lies all around, an outpost as it were of man's disputed lordship over a resentful territory. It may be that this impression holds some spiritual truth within it, for the moor is a hard land and not easily held by man, nor readily tamed to his use, and such a farm is here an outpost of agriculture in the teeth of bog and acid soil and the battering western gales.

The narrow road plunges down steeply into the valley along the scarp of the hill-face, with huge bracken-matted shoulders above and a precipitous drop below, until half a mile on it touches the bottom where a little grey bridge lifts it over the infant river. Over the stream the road turns sharply and begins to climb the opposing hill, passing between raw outcrops of jagged rock that are isles of stone torn from the hills by the storms and torrents of the centuries to stand in confusion about the valley floor, rising steadily to meet the farm above. Here now are the windbreaks of tough sycamore and beech, and here, in the midst, is the farm. The road turns sharply again, and through a gateway, and into the main yard.

The stone buildings, long, plain and slate-roofed, enclose the yard like a court. The impression of a fortress is maintained. The house backs on to one side of the yard, and the only break with tradition is that its front is turned outwards away from the farm to a garden and the sun and a wide view. Steps lead down from the yard to a door. Here to right and left the sudden unexpected brilliance of flowers in window-boxes breaks upon one, flaunting begonias, red, gold and pink, vivid against the harsh walls. The door stands open. I look in on the dignity of a hundred years ago: a long wide passageway, a hall that runs right through the width of the house to the front door, open also, under a graceful arched fanlight, giving a vista beyond of all the moor, hill and valley and long bright skyline. Pieces of fine furniture and rugs, and high on the wall a great stag's head to set the seal of Exmoor on it all. An Exmoor home, a farm of the Forest, one of the farms of the Knights, still carrying with it something of the mingled grace and solidarity of that Georgian age which gave it being.

The farm must have been built at a date some time between 1818 and 1840, in those years when the pioneering John Knight and his son Frederick were fighting to tame the wilderness of the desolate Forest that the former had bought from the Crown. Out of the waste of sedge and bent they—the Knights —carved in these years some thirteen fine farms, solid and substantial, with buildings like fortresses, grey and harsh, and houses that were big and spacious. Most of the names ring out still, bold and challenging—Horsen and Wintershead, Emmets Grange, Winstitchen, Honeymead, Red Deer, Larkbarrow, Warren, Duredon, Driver, Pinkery and Cornham. The big stretches of land were enclosed by stone walls that run still like blue serpents across the moor, and good sound roads were made from farm to farm and out to the world beyond. New breeds of beast came in colonies to the new-taken lands, sheep and cattle from the north, and shepherds from Scotland to mind them. Attempts were made to grow corn on the heights in the first optimistic years, but here the failure was great; and so eventually the Forest farms settled down to the natural order of stock-rearing, and an existence which is that of a ranch rather than a farm.

I turn out of the yard and pass the windbreak again, a forest of shining trunks, rising from deep pools of shade, and cross a field of grass, and out through a gate, and all beyond is the rolling moor, bleached and prairie-like in the summer sun. I walk out on the great expanse for a way, and then sit down for a while in the sedge and rush. Before me the Forest rolls away in a wide tawny landscape of swelling hills and deep-rifted combes, a landscape that curves round one in an encircling panorama of high and treeless skylines. Something in the distance in the wind, I know not what, sets me alert. Straining my eyes into the far distance, I can just discern moving specks. Yes, they are horsemen, and they can have only one meaning. For a while they seem to come nearer, then they disappear and one's waiting seems fruitless save for the joy of the wind and the sky and the wonderful view. Then suddenly there are deer, a smudge of brown bodies galloping to the right and disappearing in the nearest combe. There's a holloa too, from away behind. Again I wait, and after a while the hounds come up towards me from the left. How lovely they are. They ripple up over the lion-coloured grass, surging forward, and the red coats that ride with them are vivid against the mist-blue hills of the distance. They are casting as they come, and coming right up to me. The huntsman calls out to know if I have seen the stag come over—and then they go back again still questing.

Just as they go down out of sight they give tongue, and I hear them racing away below and swinging again in an arc. Here is the stag! There he goes! A brown-gold body galloping up the hill, topped by antlers that shine in the sun, moving with that rolling yet effortless gait of the wild red deer, faster than any horse can go. The hounds are on now, running hard, and the huntsman comes galloping, and some ride behind him, hunting farmers mostly and one or two others. They go bucketing through a patch of soft ground, the wet peaty mud flying from their sucking hoofs, and are gone with the hounds.

I turn away to the west, and see them no more today, though I listen and look with hopefulness all the rest of the way. The ground ahead is rough over the heights where the sedge-tussocks stand deep in black slime, and one must watch one's footing with care. The swelling hills roll westward, a high road to the sun, and the long combes drop to the north and the sullen Forest turns its face to the sea and lowers its brow to meet the heathery commons again. Under the edge of the lowering hills, by the stream that runs down from its source in the great black bogs, by the purple shoulders of heather, a roof and a gable jut from a knot of ragged beech, and broken fencing lies in the bracken.

The shepherd's cot stands empty and deserted. The whitewash has turned grey and peels from the walls, and the door is set heedlessly ajar. Here and there the slates begin to slip from the roof. The windows are blank and sad. A raven sits on the chimney-pot and croaks, then bestirs himself to fly off at the approach of footsteps.

The enclosure that was once the little garden is ragged-hedged and broken-banked, and choked with nettles and odds and ends of abandoned rubbish. The small fields that once folded sheep and cattle are lapsing back to the moor, with only a hem of fallen wire to mark their difference, and the gates are fallen down. No one lives here now.

The cot, the little place with its sheds and small enclosures, was once the 'herding' for many miles of wild desolate moorland on which were pastured big flocks of sheep, too far out for management by the established Forest farms. Now it is abandoned because no one will live in its isolation in these progressive times. No road leads to it nor any track of discernible sort, and to make a road would be too costly in terms of modern economics. The moor surrounds it on all sides, a lapping tide, and only the ravens and foxes keep it company now. Some sheep there are still on the hill, wild Scotch Blackface, but they are strays from a farm far off down the valley.

I turn away sadly from the cot. It was a pleasant little homestead once. A small island of life and comfort in the waste, and often the orange glow from its windows must have lighted home the shepherd of the hills late about his tasks. There is always sadness in an empty and crumbling house where once there has been hearth and warmth and human hopes. Out of the very desolation of the poor little place I feel my own home call to me, and I quicken my steps away to be by my own fireside before the dusk falls fast about the empty hills.

To Shoulsbarrow on a September morning of hot sunshine and a sky blue-grey with heat.

The morning shadows reach north-west before me, and all the hills of the western moor lie golden in the sun as I come up to the long high ridge above the net of valleys. Here is a landscape prairie-like with bleaching, dry, gold grass, with tattered beech turning to umber-brown and a trackway whitening to dust, and one lonely barrow lifting above a sea of tawny rush as a landmark against the sky.

A halt to eat part of my lunch, then I go on again through the waste of bleached moor, once open but now hemmed by sheep wire, with blue distance reaching away to the west, until at last the huge blunt head of Shoulsbarrow rises and thrusts out to meet the greener hills of Devon. Its majesty is scarred by the hedge lines of enclosures, and men have struggled to tame the land about its flanks, but still its lofty crown lifts rush and heather to the sky.

As I come to the old crossroads where the hills run back to the Forest and the roadway turns left into Devon, a flock of sheep come streaming over the ridge before me, down from the moor and across into a small field where there is a hut. They are hawk-faced Cheviots, a big flock, and men on horseback are driving them with the aid of the inevitable black-and-white collies. The air is full of their bleating, and dust rises from the track as they move. They are in the field by the time I pass the gate, and the men are dismounted and busy with them. The horses are tethered to the fence, their saddles shining in the sun. The familiar hot, acrid sheep-smell fills the gateway. It is all an integral part of the tawny landscape, of sheep country.

On up the western road, where the hedges curve back from the ocean wind, and through a gate and up over thick rush ground to where a low, wind-battered hedge climbs up to run over the high skyline. The bank seems to run on into infinity and the twisted beech that crowns it cowers away from the west in shattered clumps, flayed by the Atlantic gales into strange horizontal shapes, and stunted heather seams its sides. I negotiate the sheep wire along the top, and am over, and before me are the earthen ramparts of Shoulsbarrow Castle.

The long low mound-lines, matted with heather, square out on the very apex of the wind-swept height, enclosing a large level rectangular space. I walk all round the top of the inner bank or vallum, picking my way through the tangle of heather, and at last sit down at the point which seems to command the best view over the rolling landscape below. I kick off my boots —I have already walked more than eleven miles, and have as much to walk aback—and set to eating the rest of my lunch. I think of and look first at the great spreading view below, reaching away into the blue haze of heat. Here one sits, on the last great bastion of Exmoor, looking westward across all north Devon to face the mighty Atlantic that for ever batters at Hartland Point and the long coast of Cornwall beyond. The cowering riven hedge behind tells its own story. Through the shining haze the ranging eye picks out the familiar landmarks of the lower land—all the hills and woods that rise and fall between the innumerable deep-fingered valleys, hill beyond hill, rolling fainter in the blue until one can just mark where the sea shines and where Dartmoor heaves to the sky. If the day were clearer one would see the cliffs and the tors, and between them Brown Willy far off in Cornwall. The eye comes back, nearer to the farms lying below, small and sheltered under the hills, and to the steep tangled slopes and the valley bottoms choked with woods. One looks leftwards, and there is the long tawny rampart of moor stretched out to Five Barrows, the highest westerly point of Exmoor. It is all a loneliness of rush and bent, too wind-lashed and rain-sodden even for the heather. (For the hot dry weather of the past week or so is most unusual for these Atlantic-facing hills.) Hedges and the wire fences of more modern times reach up to make enclosures as high on the flanks as is worth while, but it is still a land defiant and not willingly tamed, and a thousand years removed from the sheltered comfortable farms below.

My thoughts come back to the ancient hill fort on whose sunken walls I sit. How, when and why? Always such questions come when one sees and stands upon these works of other days and hands of long ago. I know little enough of archaeology, but it seems obvious that this was a fortress raised to command and dominate the lowland to the west. The rectangular shape would seem to argue Roman influence. May it have been a Roman outpost looking out through the salt sea wind and driving rain to the hostile Celtic west? Or a later British encampment raised against the engulfing tide of Germanic invasion? Did a people once inhabit the highlands of the moor withdrawn and defiant against the settling lowland folk? The heather blowing on the ridges gives no answer, nor the rushes in the half-filled moat. Two ravens circling overhead croak harshly. Their kind have picked human bones many times before.

This strange fortress is far from being the only one of its sort on the moor. There are many silent enigmas of sunken and crumbling banks, crowning various conical hills both around and within the region. Cow Castle, Mountsey Castle and Brewers Castle on the Barle, Road Castle above the Exe, Berry and Countisbury Castles on the north side, and Bury to the south, are some of them. They are supposed generally to date from the Iron Age, and one can assume that the ones of smaller and more irregular shape, such as Cow Castle, are the earliest. That they must have been the work of a warlike people, or at least a people used to living in a warlike state, is the most obvious thing one can say about them, and beyond this there are only silence and uncertainty.

October

THE COLOURS of October. Now in the days of the autumn month all the land blazes in the pride of colour that is the culmination of all the year, and all the seasons that have gone before. Everywhere the beech flares to the sky like flames, red and orange and gold, like a running fire along the fields; and the hills are yellow and the shadows blue and the autumn grass is greener than spring.

Here where I stand by the old yard, dreaming for a moment in the morning sunshine, the trunks of the tall trees rise like columns, like the pillars of a mighty nave, shining silver-gold from under their curtains of golden-red leaf, their long shadows reaching out across the roadway and over to the old round house that faces back at them, its slate roof tucked down like a deep blue brim about the glowing stonework of its walls. Beyond the roof more beech flames up to meet the sky that arches overhead, and by my side the splat runs singing over the stones and down the hill, and its banks are thick with emerald grass all speckled with fallen leaves like coins of copper and gold. About the tree-tops the rooks are busy with the morning, and their black wings carry them around and afar to the stubble fields where the last corn lies.

Over the hedge in the ricksplat our little corn ricks are newly thatched with rush from the bog, looking as though they had bonnets of pale green upon their golden heads. Out in the lane the ash leaves make a scattering of yellow on the grass, and the last late flowers, blue-eyed sheep's bit and sprigs of heather and a few campions, flower gaily still, reluctant to forgo the last lingering of summer.

Amongst the fallen leaves, and in the clefts of wood and mould, stranger and more lurid growths appear, strange life that has waited in darkness all the year. Now late September and October days bring forth the fungi. Now between the late summer sun and the autumn mists and rains are brought to birth all the wealth of toadstools and mushrooms, puffballs and lichens, lurid colours and scaling growths that this western land holds within its body. Everywhere, on the moor and in the woods, under the hedges and about old timber, the bright and nameless things come forth. In form and colour they delight the eye, in taste some at least are good, and if one should find a few that are poisonous, then one has only oneself to blame for meddling with them and disturbing them where they grow.

Wonderful things indeed now lurk amongst the leaves and roots. Here are great scarlet toadstools spotted with white as though with paint, and tiny ones too like red buttons, and others that are blood-red with thick orange underparts. Under the beech appear big smooth rose-pink ovals with ivory flesh, and in the banks strange shapes of vivid orange and yellow like the peel of lemons. Here you may find wide umbrellas of brown, and there curious growths of purple. From the crannies of old gateposts come forth rosettes of silk-like orange-gold, and amongst the grass are yellow puffballs like split fruits, and a dozen sorts of elves' caps. From crumbling wood come pallid things like spirits, shapes from the dim underworld, and grey and ghostly fringes seaweed-like round all the posts. Sometimes you may find forms like tongues of flame under the heather, strange and mysterious. Sometimes, if you are lucky, you may still find delicate button mushrooms in the short grass, all cream and pink in the freshness of the morning. Lichens too now wax in strength, encrusting the stones with strange florescence, and covering things with many colours. Yellow and gold and black, white and green and rust, they gild the walls and rock with the livid flowering of the autumn dampness.

Now the moor opens wide before me. The heather has sunk to a pinkish-brown, all but a few late tufts that still flaunt purple heads to the sun, and the gorse has gone for the year, but oh, the flame of the bracken on the slopes, lighting the moor with fire!

Presently the heath gives way to the Forest, where the light plays on the orange and yellow of autumn sedge, and the blue shadows fold in the long low hollows. I rest for a moment under a crumbling boundary bank, with the wind singing in the sheep-wires over my head, and two ravens, circling in the sky, draw near. Closer and lower they come, till I can see the wide-fingered feathers of their wings and the spread wedge tails, and hear the beating chug of their flight as they pass and repass just above. I like them not. Their language is horrid, and their attention vaguely disturbing. I rise and go, with the sudden peculiar realization that the moor is still a wild and lonely place.

I come down by an ancient wind-battered hedge of riven and twisted beech, and make my way downward into a deep and lonely combe, and now before me a valley opens out in splendour. Great hills clothed with red-russet bracken and seamed with indigo shadow, hills of bent pure yellow-gold in the sun or turned to blue under the passing clouds, thorn trees clinging in bright green tufts on the slopes, bleached sedge by the twisting water. One stands, bewildered by the rainbow colour and all the bright confusion. Clitters of blue-grey shale lie among the brown heather and on the valley floor little green lawns of sheep-bitten turf lie like smooth pools amongst the turbulence of russet. On a knoll in the midst an old herding-corral is set, its angular timbers the only evidence of man's hand in all this wild and lovely landscape. I go on down into a deep gully overgrown with low twisted oaks, and strike a rough path that leads by the water's edge. It winds with the stream, over shelves of rock, and on the far side a crumbling wall winds like a blue snake. There are oak woods now hanging on the hills, thickets of green-gold scrub, twisted and dwarfed into a clinging cover. The path widens, and leads to a little glade of sturdier oaks. Here is dappled shadow and smooth grass and the outline of some little enclosures. I look round and see old fallen stones about a hillock. Here surely are the remains of some little farmstead. But when and how long ago? and why its abandonment? It is but one of the smaller mysteries of the moor.

The track rises now and I walk on up to an oak thicket at the top, and there sit and rest and look back into the valley. The view is glorious and seems to hold an infinity of wonder far beyond its earthly limits. The sun is moving low and golden to the west, casting deep dark shadows along the walls of the combe. The radiant light shines through the leaves of the oak with a strange living intensity, like a presence calling to the earth. And I am Adam, looking on creation.

I walk slowly down again to the little glade and along by the singing stream, upon my long homeward journey. There are black cattle now grazing by the water, Galloways, polled and shaggy, and they look up at me, then run bounding over the heather. They seldom see a human being other than a shepherd.

The valley seems even more beautiful in the low gilding light as the long shadows of evening spill deep into it, and the thorn trees stand like figures at the water. But it is time to hurry now, before dusk comes creeping with stealth on the trail of the sun. The hard road will not be unwelcome when I come to it.

§

RAIN, RAIN, RAIN. It pours down without stopping, an unceasing sheet of wetness, all day from dawn and onwards, without the promise of the slightest break. Everything and everywhere is wet, and the things one touches are wet, and the wet finds its way down one's collar and up one's sleeves and splashes about one's boots till one's feelings are soured like the dull grey cloud above. Even the dogs decline to go out, and sulk in odd corners of house and building, while the cats have disappeared long ago. From every gutter and eave the water flaunts its triumph and spouts in glee, to drench the head of the unwary and fill the yard with unwanted pools.

What can one do on a day like this? One can always tidy the barn, I suppose. Or try to. As often as one does, some malevolent force quickly returns all things to their former confusion—only worse, because in the first state one had acquired some instinct for where certain things might be found or at least looked for, whereas in the state following the disintegration of a tidying up nothing is to be found anywhere by anyone. However, it is dry in the barn, excepting for a few odd places where the rain drips through under slipped slates, so the means may justify the end, or circumstances the reason.

What a place is a barn! A general receptacle and storehouse for everything that cannot find a home anywhere else, each and all deposited in a general and most artistic state of disorder. The threshing tackle at one end, piled hay bales at the other, sacks of meal and grain in the middle and everything else between—bags of cement and plaster (the latter split and pouring pink contents over everything else), half-empty and spilling bags of chaff, the remains of old seed potatoes, old sacks (good, torn or rotting), cans and bottles of half-used animal medicines, old pots and pans (the puppies' dining utensils), bits of metalwork of dubious origin and purpose, receptacles ranging from old baths to wicker-work baskets, old pony harness, bits of rope, a few pieces of furniture, endless quantities of empty brown-paper meal-bags, and lastly, under and over all, a deep carpet of old straw and chaff.

I make a start, largely to reassure myself that I am about to do something useful. A few things shifted from one place to another, a few sacks sorted and folded, and one can say the thing is under way. But the dust! It is as venomous within as the rain is outside, and I am soon coughing and sneezing. In transit I seem to have uncovered a flooring of massive timbers across the centre of the barn. Here surely is the old threshing-floor, the threshold that lay within the door, where once the grain was beaten from the husk in the short late autumn days before the closing winter. Here they must have threshed with flails, perhaps not so very long ago, in the days before the built-in, machine-driven thresher was installed in the lower end of the barn.

Two other curious objects, or one might say edifices, come to light from under the general debris. These big box-like contraptions are respectively a comber and dresser, the one for combing wheat-straw or 'reed' for thatching and the other for dressing out grain from the chaff-husk after threshing. They stand silent and outmoded, witnesses of the past days when every hill farm had to be self-sufficient in all things from corn to roofing. Various other objects that turn up are interesting—such as the old peat-cutting tools—but most are pure junk, the sort of thing for which one has no further use, yet which one does not throw away because it always has been there. The pony harness is pathetic, and wakes memories of clopping hoofs and candle-lamps flickering on a wet road.

All the while the rain pours down outside as though it would float the barn away like the ark. It cascades off the roof like a waterfall in spate and swills across the yard, backed now with gusts of rising wind. A journey to the house means a wild dash, like crossing a line of fire—a veritable running the gauntlet.

Time now to see sheep, weather or no weather. One clothes oneself in heavy raincoat and gum-boots like a knight putting on armour, and resolutely turns forth to the elements. The rain is coming down heavier and heavier.

It beats down in torrents, straight down like lead at first, then streaming out horizontally before the rising westerly gale, flying and stinging like hail. I tie my sou'wester down tightly and struggle out across the fields and up to 'the top'. It is one of the worst walks I have ever had. I walk blind most of the time, bent nearly double against the wind, trying to keep the stinging rain out of my eyes. The force of the wind and rain is terrific, and the sheer weight of it beats one back like a living power, tearing at one's breath and battering and confusing one. The gates once open are almost impossible to shut. I can scarcely make headway in the teeth of it, and once, for the first time in my life, think I shall have to turn back. But at last I reach the partial shelter of a hedge and turn to look along it at the sheep. The sheep are huddled in wet misery, so wet that they are like soaked sponges; and as one or the other shakes itself in desperation, the wet flies out from its fleece in a silver cloud as from a soaking mop. The landscape is hidden under a blue-grey pall of rain. Great pools like ponds are forming in any hollow parts of the field, and over the hedge the moor is a swimming morass.

The homeward journey is less of a struggle for I have the weather mostly behind me. The light is going quickly now under the heavy wrack, and night advances. Over the western hedges the clouds stream straight up from the horizon, rearing black and monstrous in the gathering dusk. Our splat is a raging coffee-coloured torrent, and the yards are filling with the water that pours off all the eaves and gutters faster than it can get away. What a night. In the little combe just below the stream is already up over the bridgeway of the lane in a churning flood. There are murmurs about 'the worst since Lynmouth night'. By the morning we shall hear tales of flooding and wreckage in the valleys.

One is thankful to live upon a hill on a night like this, and know that at least one's hearth and home and yards are above the level of any possible flood. One would not sleep so soundly if it were otherwise, and one's dwelling on lower ground, and one's fields beside a river.

One is thankful, too, to have no reason for going on a journey in such weather and on such a night. Last night was the harvest supper, and an evening out for all the farm folk for miles around, so it was well that the weather held off till today. I remember the lighted hall, and the stags' antlers decked with corn and the trailing oat-heads under the black-raftered ceiling. I remember the long tables loaded with meats and pies and all good things, and the singing of hymns round the table, and the music and dancing that followed, and the endless rounds of drinking. I remember the party breaking up at some time after two o'clock in the morning, and the cars and Land-rovers sorting themselves out in the starlight to find their way home over the tracks and lanes that pass for roads in these parts, and our own journey back along the jolting track with the trees like stage cut-outs in the headlights, and the sleepy tumblings out to open the frequent gates. A happy memory, but I am glad to be home tonight.

§

MORNING on the Forest. The late October sun shines brilliantly from a sky where white clouds soar in space, tossed by a cold west wind from the distant sea. The Forest stretches in the light high and lonely, its hills all golden to the horizon, with shadows of blue and violet and lilac playing in unceasing pattern over them. The wind ruffles the sedges and bent and clumps of rush, and sweeps over all the treeless expanse and over the black bogs that lie under the matted moss, and licks at the sheep wire on the crumbling, stone-faced banks and ripples the pools that lie in the hollows of the ancient gateways. It is cold despite the sun.

The sun moves up into the zenith, and then over into the west, while we wait on the hilltop. Our senses are keen and tense as we watch every slope and combe, and listen for any sound in the wind and sweep the distant skylines with the powerful glasses. At last we see him, just for a moment, down in the valley below, by the water.

Down by the water where the long combes meet, where the storm-stripped rocks are sculptured like castles, the big stag comes with quickening pace. For far behind him—yet not so far—he hears the cry of the hounds, intermittent, but persisting and unyielding. He is a big stag indeed, an old stag—one of seven that were roused this morning from the deep fern beds above the Exe. He is the last stag of the year, for today is the last day's hunting of the season. Already he is a rutting stag, thick-necked and short-tempered, ready to roar in the moonlight. He is a dark beast, grizzled black under the rufous back, with a thick ruff of grey beard falling about his neck; and the antlers he carries are long and sweeping and black, the twelve points polished white at the tips. 'All his rights and three'.

He splashes into the water and out again, and turns up the hill in a long slanting arc, and over the open height to head for the farther valley. The long valley opens before him, and he comes down to water again, down through bracken and sedge and thickets of stunted thorn to the blue rocks by the pools where the wild duck rise. But still the hounds are behind, and coming nearer now. He tries the water, and beats down to the cover of the little wood in the throat of the valley. Still the hounds come, the huntsman riding with them, encouraging them and lifting them, his red coat a splash of blood in the sun.

The dark stag turns again. He will make a last try for the big oak woods that lie beyond the hills that roll down to the northern sea. He leaves the water and turns up the hill that is as steep as the roof of a house, up over shale and scree, up through the stunted scrub oak that clings like a beard on the rim. He reaches the top, labouring now, but a new deer fence faces him, the handiwork of some over-efficient farmer who has sought to guard a new-sown ley against the depredations of the wild. He turns back and drops down a little goyal, back to the running river. A holloa, and a crash of hound music. They see him now, and hounds are running in view, and there are horsemen riding like men-at-arms on the skyline.

He turns yet again, back up the little stream that runs narrow but deep under shelves of rock, all hung with ferns and tussocks of heather. He is in the water and the hounds are behind him. A little grey bridge bars his way. He can only turn and face them now, head high, and they are all around him.

The red coat rides down with thundering hoofs, a group of hunting farmers close behind. They swing from their sweating horses. There's the sound of a shot. It is over now. The brown body sinks down into the water, stained with blood. The hounds drop wearily into the heather.

Willing hands draw the heavy body, dark with sweat and water, from the stream and lay it on the grass. More riders are coming down now and several Land-rovers and a few people on foot. They press around and admire the fine head and pluck little tufts of hair from the shaggy beard for the memory of a good run and a noble beast. The huntsman has taken off his red coat and attends to the last act. The slots are struck off and presented, the carcass disembowelled in a welter of blood, and the hounds called for their reward. They come in a snarling wave of white and tan, and the horn sounds in long notes over their feast. It is a ritual as old as the Dark Ages, like an ancient scene of sacrifice, the seal of triumph of man the hunter.

It is finished. The hounds go home in the long light of the western sun, and the jingle of bits and spurs goes with them. Another day, another season ended. The rowan tree by the bridge shakes in an eddy of wind that comes down the combe, and forest and hill wait for the night, and the deer for the autumn moon.

§

THE THICK white mist of early morning lifts slowly from the hills, withdrawing before the golden rays of the autumn sun until at last all the sky is a clear bright blue from rim to rim, and all the moor lies revealed in October light.

It is well that the day is fair and fine, for today is the day of the drift, the annual pony-gathering on the moor. Since first morning, before the lifting of the mist, the riders on horseback have been out driving the combes and hidden gullies, rousing the ponies from their grazing places, setting them running from the thickets of gorse and deep bracken beds and sending them out and away over the rough heather and splashing bog.

Down by the river where I stand there is silence except for the running water, and the hills look blue against the sun. Then suddenly there are shouts and holloas out of the distance and horsemen appear on the skyline, set against the light like cut-out centaurs. For a moment they stand, and then they are gone down into the far combe. Now there are more horsemen, nearer, galloping through the bracken. One of them is looking and holloaing up the river. There go the ponies—dark forms, small and far off, plunging through the river where the old ford lies and moving up over the big heather-brown side of the moorland beyond. Following them up are the riders who have pushed them over the river. One's blood seems to kindle at the sight. Horses in herds drifting like deer over a wild bare hillside, like a sight from an olden world. It is as if one sees again the bands of wild horses drifting over a limitless prairie and hears again the shouts of the hunters of the great long ago.

All the riders are across the river now, following up the drift, spreading out on the flanks to prevent any breakaway, curving the herd eastwards to the pound, driving the ponies ever inwards to the one place. There are shouts from the hillside and horsemen galloping, as some of the ponies try to break from the main drift, but are headed back. On the hill where the enclosure hedges gather together is the long neck of moor that is the gathering pound, and I hurry up the hill to be there just before they come.

Now the drift is coming in. A drumming of hoofs like muffled thunder and a racing stream of red-brown bodies pouring, flowing, surging, like a wave through the heather and gorse and bent, with holloaing riders galloping on the flanks. The long wave rushes on, wheels, is headed and pressed in by the horsemen, and then runs headlong into the pound space. Someone sounds a hunting horn, and the riders rein their sweating horses and close the gap in a long file. So they come again, the little wild horses of Exmoor, as they have done since first they fled before the hunter in the days when all things were wild.

Held in the space between the high hedge and the long wall, barred at one end by gates and at the other by mounted men, the ponies mill and shift in a tight-packed herd. Wild as hawks, they toss and eye the banks and gates for a possible breaking-place. Mares, foals, yearlings and the high-crested stallion—they all have the mealy nose of their race, the small prick-ears, the flaring nostril, the wild bright eye. Few of them have ever been handled by man, save once at their branding.

Now begins the business of parting out. Several of the most knowledgeable farmers are afoot amongst them, reading the brands so that each man may know his own. Then by skilful manœuvring the ponies are parted out, some being turned through one gate and some through another, every mare with her foal, until every beast is claimed and each little herd is gathered to itself.

The morning wears on. The parting is a lengthy business. But at last it is done, and one by one the little groups of ponies clatter down the lanes or across the fields, close-herded by their owners, each to its own farm, to abide there for the sorting and branding.

Now the moor is left empty for a while, lonelier than ever, until the mares are turned back to the common again in a few days' time. For a while silence seems to press on it, and one feels it lies waiting for those small unshod hoofs to come up the lane and out to its space once more.

PONY-BRANDING and a wet day. In the driving rain of early morning we struggle to make-ready the yard for the coming rodeo, if so one may call it. With busy hands bits of iron rail are set above the gates and tied into position, and old hay-lades are wedged in odd places. Sheep wire is staked into position along the top of the garden bank. All the usual assorted debris of a farmyard—old bits of broken implements, forgotten tools, bits of timber, sacking, rope or chain—is for this one day in the year collected up and put somewhere else. It is as though we were converting the yard into an arena for wild beasts. Which is perhaps not so far from the truth as it sounds.

At last the thing is done as well as can be, and farmer and shepherd ride out to bring in the ponies from the adjacent field, where they have lain the night. The rest of us are stationed at strategic points—in the lane to turn the ponies into the yard, and in the yard at corners where the ponies might attempt to leap out over.

There's a muffled drumming of hoofs that changes to a rattle as flying feet meet the stone of the lane, and a voice shouts, 'They're coming'. Then a wave of brown bodies pours headlong into the yard and, trapped, turns upon itself in milling confusion.

They fill the yard, these surging, terrified wild things from the moor. Their bodies are black with rain and mud splashed, and their mealy noses stand out like stars at night. Bay, brown or dun are no longer to be distinguished or scarcely so, for all are turned to the one dark colour by the wet. Mares, yearlings, and suckers, they mill and turn about, fearful and wild-eyed, close-packed in the ring of walls and men. Few of them have ever had a halter on in their lives, except on the day they were branded, and their first and only instinct is escape. The older mares survey the gates and any likely points with calculating glances. Each of us with a post to guard, a particular weak point in the defences, draws close to it.

Now comes the moment of concerted effort necessary to force the ponies into the long stable and shippon. All hands close round the ponies and try to head them into the open doorways. But into the dark buildings they will not go if they can help it;

time and again they break away and race from end to end of the yard, ever seeking a way of escape, churning the mud of the yard into a flying froth. How lightning-quick Exmoors can turn! They shy and wheel away from the open doors in a flash, their hoofs clashing on the cobbles. Two ponies are knocked off their feet in the *mêlée* and one turns a somersault. Pandemonium. Whips cracking, everybody shouting, dogs shut away in sheds barking as though the end of the world was at hand. Suddenly a seven-year-old mare, a noted breaker, plunges up the hay-yard bank in a stupendous jump and bursts through the barricade at the top. Two others follow her in a flash, and three wet brown bodies go over the top into the hay-yard, over the big drop-jump into the field beyond, and away—they are gone for the day. The jumping power of a 12 h. 2 Exmoor is phenomenal. Such a pony can and will leap a five-bar gate from a standstill.

At last one old mare, wise in things, decides that life might possibly be more peaceful inside the building than out, and slides through one of the open doors. After some persuasion the rest consent to follow, no doubt thinking likewise. The doors are closed, and we ourselves look for momentary shelter, for the rain still beats relentlessly down, and we are soaked.

The branding party arrives about midday. Excitement prevails as the Land-rovers are seen struggling up the muddy rocky lane, and in the house the kitchen stove is stoked up ready for the branding-irons. At last all is in order. The secretary of the Exmoor Pony Society sits on the barn doorstep with studbook register and the brand-heads, and the committee prepare to look at the young stock. The stable door is opened and the handlers squeeze into the mass of ponies. One by one the foals, or suckers as we usually call them, are caught and dragged forth struggling to the light. Each is inspected and if approved as being of true type, the name and number of sire and dam are then called out, also the sex—colt or mare-colt; the word filly is not often used by Exmoor men—and the youngster is given a name and a number and entered in the register.

Meanwhile the branding-irons have been getting hot and are now ready. Two men hold the little beast against the wall by head and tail, while a third shears away the hair on near-side shoulder and quarter, leaving two small bare patches. Now the branding-irons are brought red hot from the kitchen fire as called for. One at a time they are applied sharply and firmly to the skin for a few seconds. There is a sudden smell of burning hair and skin, but the creature does not seem to suffer any real pain—probably it is too terrified and bewildered to be conscious of anything—and anyway it is soon over and lard is rubbed into the burn to heal it. The society's star-brand goes on the shoulder, with the herd number under it, and the individual number goes on the quarter, sometimes in conjunction with the owner's private brand if he has such.

The last colt to be branded is a yearling who for some reason got overlooked last year. He is a strong fellow now and puts up a good fight, plunging and rearing and trying to evade the halter, and when at last he is caught it takes three grown men all their strength to hold him.

During the proceedings someone has left the top half of the stable door open for a moment. Inside, the mare nearest to it takes a leap at the door, rearing straight up from her hocks. It is a difficult jump from and through so cramped and confined a space and under a low ceiling. She hooks her forelegs over the high half-door like a cat, and then draws her belly up over with a wriggle and is out and away. I would never believe that a horse could do this if I had not seen it, and certainly none but an Exmoor would attempt it. Yet a friend tells me that an Exmoor has been known to come out through a small window high up in the same way, so apparently this is a peculiar Exmoor trick.

Everything is finished now, except for the parting out of the various ponies according as to whether they are to go back to the moor, stay 'in ground' or be sent for sale at Bampton Fair. Those that go back to the hill will have their long tails cut against the coming winter and the danger of snow. The fair will be the third day from now, the last Thursday in the month, but I care little for Bampton on a fair day, with all the jostling dealers and the terrified ponies crammed into high-walled pens, and noise and people and traffic everywhere, and would rather stay at home.

November

GREY SKIES and hills that are purple-blue beyond the long
black-headed hedges, pale bleached fields, slopes of spent and
soaking bracken, the first calls of the winter birds down the
wind that swings to the north, and frost on the morning grass.

The days of mid November come coldly after the brilliance
of the preceding weeks. The leaves are down from the higher
hedges, scattering in brown carpets on the ground; the last
flowers are spent, all but a very few in odd corners; the wind
has a cold edge to it, and the nights are growing long and the
afternoons short and fading. The last corn has come in, and our

potatoes are dug and clamped. The staghounds have finished their season and soon will be hunting hinds. Summer is gone and is only a memory now.

In our yards there is already a scattering of bright straw and wisps of dropped hay on the cobbles, for the days are come when the beasts must have food, and soon the cattle will be lying in, first the cows and calves, and then as many of the bullocks as the shippons will hold. Many birds flutter down for the seeds that are fallen, and for anything else they can find. Against the grey sky the roof of the barn is yellow with lichen, each old slate clothed with bright sulphur, golden yellow as though it had burst into curious flower; and the walls beneath are mottled too with the strange bright patterning.

Across the fields, where the grass is bitten short like a pale empty lawn, the ewes are with the ram. Tupping time has come again, and the bright colours of the reddle, vivid blue and scarlet, splash the broad chests of the rams, and the rumps of the first of the ewes. How impressive are the Exmoor rams with their great and splendid horns. The huge growths spread out and down about the face in massive curves, and then up and out again in a great corkscrew, reaching out to a span of perhaps a yard's width. In an old mature ram so massive are the horns that they seem to weigh the head down, so that one has the impression that it is an effort for the beast to raise its head at all. They are like figures from a biblical story, these mighty-headed rams, recalling to one the picture-books of childhood, and the tale of the ram caught in the thicket.

The horned Exmoors are not the only rams in the fields, though. There are others whose purpose it is to provide cross-bred, early-fattening lambs from the hardy hill ewes. Dorset Downs, big fellows with black noses and lilac ears and black-booted legs; Border Leicesters, as white-faced and Roman-nosed as Spanish chargers; tall Cluns to bring the hoped-for twins, and the local Closewools, who differ not very much from the Exmoors save for the lack of horns. On the fertility of these rams depends the whole economy of the hill farm. The undetected failure of a ram can be near-disaster for a small hill farmer. Little wonder that in the pastoral communities of ancient times the virile ram was a sacred symbol and his horned head the adornment of the altars of the gods.

I turn away across the fields and out to the moor, where the rush is bleached white and the heather sunk into the brown of winter. A group of ponies move out with raised heads from a thicket of gorse. Their winter coats are grown now and they look more than ever like little wild horses as they move through the scrub and rush. Their coats are thick like heavy velvet, and their chins are bearded. Their colouring is rich and dark— mahogany red to black-brown, in perfect harmony with the russets and dark colours of the winter landscape; but in contrast the mealy nose and belly parts are almost flour-white, like the sharpness of an oriental painting. One might paint them now in the flat and shadowless manner of the East, bringing forth the wonderful contrast and gradation of rich colour.

Below the moor the river runs swift and full at the feet of the hills. The thickets of oak and hazel above the banks have shed their leaves—all but a few clinging flecks of yellow—and the ghostly green lichen takes possession of them as though some god of the underworld had breathed strange life into them with the damp breath of the earth. The great shoulders of the hills that rise to the grey sky are cloaked with sodden bracken, red like the hide of a beast, a deep and sullen red that presses on the heights like a weight, and the folds of the combes are filled with purple shadow. On a tongue of soggy ground white with rush a herd of bullocks graze knee-deep in the waste, impressive as buffalo, living red to match the hills above.

I turn down the track that leads to the river ford and make for the crossing. The river runs full and cold as I kick off my boots and roll my trousers up to the thigh, and it flows wide to the margins under the hanging sallows. Now one must have resolution, for the water is strong. I thrust down with my hazel stick and wade. The water bites like icy jaws, and the stones of the bottom are slippery and hard to one's feet. But the far bank grows nearer now, and behold, dry land is under my feet again.

The rise from the valley is stiff and steep, and one goes slowly up the rutty path beside the rocks that jut like fangs from under the bracken upon the hill. At last I am over the shoulder and make my way down the more gradual slope towards some fields, and in the direction of some houses that lie on the lower ground.

Suddenly, suddenly there's a wild distant cry on the wind, exciting, thrilling and unmistakable. Hounds! Foxhounds, running hard. They are coming towards me, down to the cottage by the road in the hollow amongst the fields. Yet there are no riders, no horsemen anywhere. The pack must have run right away from their huntsman, and be hunting on their own, baying like the whist-hounds of the ancient tales. And running a race with their quarry too, to judge by their voices down the wind.

Across the small fields the cry of the hounds comes louder and fiercer, deepening now to a bay as they run down under the criss-cross of hedges and little paddocks behind the buildings in the hollow. Like avenging angels they course him, the thief of hens and killer of lambs, over the banks and across the plats, and into the last little field. I run and reach the gate just as they come pouring into the midst in a snarling wave. Whoop! They have him! Like a wave of the sea they pour over themselves and surge in a snarling mass of white and tan and black, a swirl of animal bodies in savage splendour on the grass.

Then the tumbling pack loosens and slackens itself, and hounds draw back from the vortex, satisfied; and out from the midst comes one hound, a young bitch, and in her jaws she carries the mask red and grinning like a trophy of war. None dares take it from her, and she carries her prize into the grass alone.

A few people appear from the nearby houses, but of the field itself there is no sign. Hounds must have run hard without a check for many miles so to out-distance even their huntsman. I come away and back up the old familiar lane towards home. The fallen leaves scuffle in the gutters, and a few last nuts and berries cling in sheltered places to provide an excuse for loitering on the way.

Presently there is a clack of hoofs on the road and the brightness of scarlet between the hedges. The huntsman comes at last, riding in search of his hounds. 'They've killed behind the houses.' 'I know', says he with that wonderful intuitive knowledge of a true huntsman, and goes on quickly down the lane. I too bestir myself to hurry now in my opposite direction, for the late afternoon is cold and growing dusky, and all things go home at eventide.

Once home, though, the day is not ended. One of the bullocks is missing and cannot be found, and so, mindful of the ancient mine-shafts deep in the woods, we decide to organize a search party. So it's off into the cold dark night with staves in hand and lanterns swinging. The way down the dark squelching fields seems like going to the ends of the earth, and the bitter night wind makes one huddle in the heavy overcoat. The long search along the endless hedges and down steep bracken slopes and through the woods is a strange and eerie progress, yet at times wonderfully beautiful, as the strong but circumscribed light of the lantern touches and plays upon the trees like an arc-light upon a stage setting, and all the branches hung with pale lichen and trails of Spanish moss are weirdly lovely and quite unearthly. We go careful of our ankles in rough places, and all the while part and meet again so as to cover as much ground as possible, each glad when our ways take us out of the bitter wind. How a lantern in the fields comes towards you out of space and darkness like a disembodied thing, floating to meet you as though without human agency. And how elusive cattle are to find at night. They never seem to be in places where one might expect to find them. At last one stumbles on some of them, almost literally, for the black and red are practically invisible and only the horns show up whitely. Then some more, then much counting and more searching, and then at last the tally is correct—the missing beast must have returned from somewhere to join its companions—and gathering ourselves together we go home with easy minds to the warm kitchen and hot soup.

§

THE SOFT west breeze comes sweet again as I go down the hill with the mare, sweet and mild after the week of bitter cold and the wild dark wind from the north. In the warmth of the low morning sun I remember the successive days of biting wind blowing straight from the eye of the north, as cold and cutting as a knife-blade, and the dark skies of blue-black cloud piling up, yet no rain falling, until one began to wonder if a great snowstorm was riding on the back of the wind. I remember trying to pick a few last, late blackberries, and my fingers so numb and aching with the cold that I could barely hold the pickings. I remember one night so dark that it was nothing but inky pitch blackness, the darkest night I have ever known, when, used though I am to the night, even my cat's eyes could see nothing about me. It was as though I were blind, and with the northern gale roaring overhead it was impossible to hear even the running of the stream by which to get my bearings. I remember finding my way up the fields, trying to steer by the wind, blundering into things under the hedges and identifying them by feel and so judging my whereabouts. And oh, the sense of relief to be home at last, with light and warmth again. Nights so truly dark are very rare, and this is the only time I have ever been benighted.

But the black wind has gone, and the hills lie in soft late autumn sunshine. The beech leaves smoulder still like sullen fire under the hedges in the lane, and the mountain-ash trees, stripped bare, shine silver in the light, and there is moss like green stockings on the boles. Flocks of small birds, fieldfares and redwings and many that I do not know, fly from hedge to hedge, all twittering, and the young mare starts and tosses her head all the way. Life is full of joy again.

Now we are down to the forge again, in the village by the Exe. Once more I stand in the smithy, under the arching doorway, looking in upon that scene beheld so many times, and which through all the ages has evoked the wonder and imagination of men. The glowing, hooded fire, the hearth before it like a sacrificial altar, the stone trough with the water winking back the flame, and in the midst the anvil, strange and potent form. Fire and water, stone and iron, elements of the elemental earth—little wonder that since man first found the use of metal and the means to bend it to his will the smith has been held in all mythologies as a magician possessed of magic powers, and still seems a sorcerer about his trade. Even now nothing of the scene has changed between this day and five-and-twenty centuries ago. The iron heated and molten in the burning fire, quenched in water with hissing steam, heated again red hot and burned on the hoof in a cloud of sizzling, acrid smoke, hammered on the anvil with the clink and clank of iron meeting iron, and then as a shoe nailed by hand and hammer to the foot of a horse. Still it is marvellous enough. Here in the half-gloom with the winking eye of the fire beyond, if I should turn and see a sword blade thrust through the iron heart of the anvil,

I would not be a whit surprised, or think it other than a natural wonder.

The forge is full: at least there are as many horses as there are spaces for tying, and I must wait my turn. Blacksmithing is a busy trade still in these parts, for this is a horseman's country, and riding the only serviceable way of crossing many a stretch of the moor. There are shepherds' ponies to shoe, farmers' hunters and other folks' hacks, and the hunt-horses from the kennels, and one or two draught-horses as well. Shoeing is very much a matter of appointment over the phone in these crowded days.

At last there is a space for my horse, and seeing her settled I can go and be about my other errands. The sunshine calls, and my way takes me up the winding river valley. The scattered houses drop away one by one, and soon there is only the flowing water for company.

A short way on I stop awhile and lean over a favourite gate just where the road turns up the hill, and gaze up over the grassy slopes to the heights of the moor that rise to close the narrowing valley. Then I turn and retrace my steps and the sun sends shafts of dazzling light and bars of dappled dancing shadow across my eyes. Somewhere a missel-thrush sings from a tree.

Shoeing is a lengthy business, and the way home is long, and the sun hangs low in the sky by the time we reach the foot of the ancient pack-horse track and start our last ascent to home. A stop half way for a breather, for the way is steep, and a few moments snatched to look out over the wide and spacious view and to marvel at the wonder of all creation.

The high moor is very lovely in the late afternoon sunshine, with the woods running up to it all glowing golden and shadowed with blue and lilac colour. As one mounts up to the hills one looks out over the land and sees the pattern of hedge-banks lying like a net over it, and one sees underneath the immemorial contours of hill and valley, curved and shadowed, carved by the ages of wind and rain and sun. The hand of man touches only the surface, and as it has been so it may be again. To the west the long ridges sink into the vast golden radiances of light, themselves dissolving into light. Nearer at hand there are peacock-blue shadows on the sides of the combes.

The sun sinks and turns red and the red ball disappears behind the rim, and soon it will be twilight and night again. I hurry now, for I am hungry and there is hot supper waiting. The dogs too will have a feast tonight, for the crows killed a hogg this morning. It must have got on its back in the night, for by dawn light they had torn the underparts to pieces, ripping the belly and picking the head to the bone in a gory mess. It is a loss to lose a good young sheep thus, but in these parts we offset the loss somewhat by skinning the carcass and feeding the flesh to the dogs.

§

A WET MORNING at the beginning of winter, and a wet walk up the hill. The deep narrow lane runs up the hill steeply and straight, as though it had a purpose in mind, though what that purpose might be it must have long ago forgotten, for on reaching the top it comes to an abrupt end at a gate that opens only to the empty moor.

The rain drops softly from the branches of the arching beech hedges that almost meet overhead, turning the lane in parts to a tunnel, and goes to swell the rivulets that run overflowing from a score of little springs rippling down the sides of the roadway in miniature torrents. Fallen leaves make small sodden drifts to clog the running water here and there. Deep green moss cushions the crumbling banks, clinging between the thin, blue-grey stones of old dyking, and clothing the rootstocks of the beech. Long fronds of last summer's ferns hang in soaking tresses of rich chestnut-brown over earth and stone, and tight in the crevices the fat pennyworts swell with the rain. The tough brambles that arch out from the tangle still bear leaves of rich dull purple, wine-red and dusky green, and trailing tufts of old grass make patches of bleached yellow amongst them.

As the lane climbs the spine of the hill, scored deep into the rock, gateways open at intervals on either hand, like windows in a corridor, giving vistas of small wet green-dun fields under a grey heaven, and deeper tangled woods below, and farther off a hint of grey hills through the misty rain. A gateway in an

Exmoor lane is always a window at which one instinctively stops to look out and beyond the narrow confines. I stop now by a gateway near the top of the hill and lean upon the wet gate, hot and glad to linger for a while (for the sou'west weather is almost warm, and it is heavy walking uphill in raincoat and gumboots). Looking out across the narrow combe below I can see the rust-red roof of our lower linhay, small and squat in a corner of hedges between the steep brown slopes and the smoother fields above, and I can hear the noise of the running stream below.

From the arch of the lane there comes another sound. The sound of hoofs and a voice and a swirl of movement. Hounds! Down the hill they come, a wave of tan and white, flickering sterns, a flash of red coats, and the voice of the huntsman calling them on. A breath-like steam rises in a mist from the hot bodies as they pass and the smell of sweating horses goes with them. Then the clatter of more hoofs, and horsemen, some dozen of them, following on. Ringing hoofs, jingling bridles and spurs, the rasp of leather, the splendour of bone and muscle and straining animal power—riders upon horseback. How they stir the blood on a grey winter morning!

They turn down through a gate, and go down into the rough valley below, cross to the other side, and disappear into the woods. I wait and watch hopefully for a little while, but they draw away up the combe and do not come back, so at length I resume my walk.

Presently I come to another rough and winding lane, descending into a narrower, tangled combe with a little rushing stream cascading down beside it. The road, grass-grown, begin to rise on the farther side, and above, masked by beech trees, are the outbuildings of a farm, gaunt and grey like the bastions of a castle. Another sudden bend, a steeper ascent, a gate, and one is in the yard. Grey weathered buildings, low doorways, stone steps leading up to lofts, glimpses of moorland between the roofs—just another hill farm. After some conversation with my farmer friend I am taken into a large dimly lit box. There is a snort and a wild scuffle of hoofs and a pony shies into the corner, wheeling round to face us with all the suspicion of a wild thing. As my eyes get used to the imperfect light I see him more clearly. A three-year-old stallion colt of one of the oldest

Exmoor herds, fresh in from the moor. Wild as a bird, un-haltered, unbroken, untamed, starting and wheeling, cowering belly down like a dog at every human movement—here is a true wild horse! He is fox-red, darkening to black points, and his mealy nose shows up like a light. He is strong and clean and well-made all over, and I should judge him to be about 12 h. high.

I sit on the rungs of the loft-ladder, and take out my painting things and begin to work as well as I can in the poorish light. He watches me, breathing heavily all the while with nervous tension, and starts at my every slight movement. Gradually he gets a little more used to my presence, and begins to snatch at his hay. At last I have some sort of likeness, and rise stiffly from the ladder to find my legs again.

The rain continues, a steady drizzle, into the afternoon. I resume my walk, and eventually arrive home. Everything is a welter of mud, and it seems as if nothing will ever dry up. Water, water, everywhere, is true enough.

Then towards late afternoon the sun breaks through and the clouds suddenly disperse, giving a most lovely end to the day. The sky becomes an arc of china blue, suffused with gold and curdled over with a little freckled cloud. All the myriad rain-drops are turned by the westering sun to showers of golden diamonds, and every tree trunk glistens in the light. It is magical, like walking in paradise, and the mud and the rain are all forgotten.

§

An afternoon that is spring before its time. The sun shining over rising white-topped clouds fills the little valley with clear golden light, brightens the steep hillsides and sets the stream sparkling with a thousand points of light. Its soft warmth is like a breath held in a bowl.

The little river runs full, steel-bright and foaming over its bed of rock, singing with the voice of the moor. The sound of the water fills my ears with the swelling ceaseless song, splash-ing, rippling, muttering—and its eternal flowing movement, without beginning or end, mesmerizes the senses with an utter timelessness. Three old gnarled alders cling to the bank and bend forward over the water, their black branches soon to put forth a myriad of catkins, dusky pink against the dark rough bark. The sun gilds the brown rushes at my feet, and is warm on my hands.

A little grey bridge spans the water where it turns under the hill, its three arches all grown green with moss like patches of velvet thrown across it, and two tall firs, old spruces, stand sentinel at one end. The rough stony road that runs over its back leads only to a lonely farm high up on the edge of the moor. Nothing comes this way to disturb the peace of the valley save the truck from the farm and perhaps the red mail-van in the early morning.

Just beyond the stream, reaching to it, and bounded by a broken wall, is a little green meadow. Here a small group of Devon steers, dark red, white-horned beasts, out-wintered, graze in the narrow piece of valley pasture.

All around the hills close in, rough with bracken or smooth with grass, girded with tall beech hedges, bright in the sun or folded with shadow. It is so very lovely that I feel contented and loath to go. The little bridge holds the eye like the centre-piece of a picture. How pleasing a thing is a bridge, at once useful in purpose and graceful in structure—a work of architecture and a symbol of travel. With what skill its stones are set to arch above the dashing water, meeting nature on an equal level of stress and strain, obeying in its own way the same laws of force and gravity as govern the running stream. Long ago an ancient chronicler listened to the sound of all the singing rivers of the moor, and called the country 'the land of many waters', and even as it is so, it is also a land of many bridges. Big and little, they carry the roads from the hills over the waters of many a valley and combe.

These, our grey bridges that leap across the hurrying streams, have many sizes according to need, though little difference in sort. The smallest kind have but one arch, often so small that one would have to bend double to splash through, though one or two that I know have a good springing span, and a few bridges have two arches. Next after these come the triple-arched bridges that take the water in three strides with but-tressed piers between; and lastly there are the great ones with five or six arches. Whatever their size they are all alike of rough moorstone, plain and purposeful, devoid of any ornamentation, and seem a natural part of the hilly scene and rocky streams.

The oldest Exmoor bridges date from late medieval times, when they were built for the convenience of the pack-horse trains at those points on the cross-country routes where the river-crossings were deep and dangerous in winter spate. The finest of all these pack-horse bridges is undoubtedly Landacre, which spans the Barle midway between Withypool and Simonsbath, and which is on the line of the old track westwards to Barnstaple. Five fine arches, buttressed against the uncertain flow of the river, step across from rocky scarp to marshy rise, with all the loneliness of the moor and hill for a background. The parapets are very low along the narrow length, low enough for the packs and panniers to swing above them, and still one may think one sees the pack-ponies coming when one hears the clash of hoofs on the road above the bridge.

A fine single-arched bridge, little known now, is that which springs across the Exe at Lyncombe below Exford. It rises in the middle to a slight point, and is very narrow indeed. Today it seems but to lead from one side of a farmyard to another, for the highway that it once served is now a forgotten track scarcely discernible amongst the gorse and bracken of the hills. The better-known bridge at Malmsmead is a good example of a two-arch type, while the bridge at Simonsbath, though probably later in date, is fairly typical of the triple-arched sort.

The big bridge at Withypool, a very beautiful one of six arches, can be classed as modern, as it is less than a hundred years old, and local men can tell how their grandfolk remember its building. It was, I believe, built entirely with local materials by local labour, and is an example of the continuity of a building tradition unimpaired by alien influence.

The great flood of 1952, when all the rivers came down in spate like boiling furies, took many bridges with it as it swept on its course of destruction; yet most of the older ones stood up to it well, which may be taken as a tribute to the unknown builders of former times. After the flood the fallen bridges were slowly rebuilt and the damaged ones repaired, and one bridge in particular—that near Watersmeet—which was rebuilt by a local firm, is a very beautiful structure indeed, proving that modern workmanship can still equal the best of past ages when allowed to do so.

If our bridges are many, though, they are yet not so many as the fords, their predecessors at the ancient river-crossings. There are many hundreds of known fords at all parts of the moor, across all the many waters—horsemen's fords, but most of them negotiable also by horse and cart, and by folk on foot. Quite a number still exist across the now metalled highways, through which the modern motorist must voyage and pray that they are not too deep-running. On the whole, and in normal times, the local fords are not deep—though if on foot one should always remember that the hill streams run with great force and tug—but in time of spate they should always be treated with great respect, not only because of unaccustomed depth and force, but because the bed beneath may have been torn out and rendered treacherous.

But time waits for no man, and I must be going. So a walk in golden sunshine up over the hill, with a halt at the top, to look back at the tawny moor in the west. The long ridge runs all gold and blue-shadowed under the sky, with a great hammer-headed cloud rearing up behind it, the long green fields of the high farm below it, and the clustered farm set white in the middle. The distant farm shows walls and roofs as sharp-cut as toys on a green patchwork cloth, and there are bullocks in the fields like tiny red miniatures. Eastwards the waste of rush moor is an orange sea billowing to violet-silver horizons. The sun sinks, and the strange sweet scent of the bogs hangs on the evening air. Somewhere a bird is piping, and a waxing moon rises to light me home.

§

THE OPEN moor and a sou'west gale. Since before dawn the wind and rain have battered and torn at all the land with the fury of a western storm. Now the road before me stretches away into seeming infinity, a narrow ribbon that rises and falls and twists, shining with the running wetness of the storm, but hard and sure in a world of bog and rain-mist. It runs on, turning about the contours of the hills, elbowing around the head of some combe, disappearing and reappearing, yet always going on, swept by the driving rain that billows like smoke across it, on over the lonely empty miles that are without shelter or habitation. To right and left the dark moor rolls back in the sullen desolation of winter, shrunk into itself under the lashing of the wind—a dark land that drops to hidden rivers, and rises again from between the long fingers of the combes like the swell of a turbulent sea, hill beyond hill, grey heaving ridges reaching to a featureless horizon under a grey heaven of tearing tattered cloud.

The wind batters at everything, flattening the heather and rush and bending and shaking the gorse. The rain drives everywhere, soaking and relentless. Walking into the teeth of it one can scarcely make headway, and is glad to rest for a moment where the road dips a little at the head of a goyal and the full force of the wind is slackened for a small space. Here a spring breaks from a patch of bog above the road, and frothing white water spills down over cushions of yellow sphagnum moss, down into the goyal where cowering black thorns cling and crouch among the sodden red of last year's bracken, hurrying to join the already swollen streams.

Out across the shoulder of the hill a small flock of Blackface sheep graze stubbornly, their drooping, tow-coloured fleeces white amidst the wet brown of the heather, and those nearest to hand lift their horned mottled heads to gaze at me wonderingly. They are the only life in a desolate world.

They fit well into this storm-swept landscape, these northern sheep, so far from their Highland home. They seem as though they belonged to the land like the thorn trees and the ancient rowans, presenting a traditional moorland picture. Yet in point of fact it is only in the last few years that they have become established here on the heather wastes of Exmoor. There is no doubt about their hardiness, and they alone of all sheep are expected to winter on the open moor, though even they do not always survive. The wool and mutton they produce are not as good as that of the native Exmoor, but in their favour it is said that they will live mostly on the shoots of the heather, with less dependence on grass than most other breeds of sheep.

But it is no time or place to linger. The rain drives deeper and wetter into one and the wind is exhausting. Somewhere over the skyline on the far side of the high land there are beech hedges and shelter; and somewhere still farther off there are farmsteads and homes. One turns again into the wind and goes forward with urging thoughts of a fire and hot dinner and rest in dry clothes and talk with friends.

The beech hedges at last, bent and roaring in the wind. Oh, the blessed shelter of them! And here is the crossroads just under the moor, lonely and trafficless. The staghounds should be here this morning, if they can face the weather. It is worth a short wait to see if they come.

The sharp clatter of shod hoofs on the hard wet road, heard through the deafening sound of the beech—they come. Huntsman and whipper-in bent forward in their saddles to meet the wind, their scarlet hidden under the long dun-coloured raincoats, their horses slippery with the wet and the hounds mud-splashed and trotting on between them. They rein and turn in under the lee of the hedge, pressing their horses' quarters back tight to the bank to gain a little shelter. The hounds crowd into the ditch. A little while, and three more riders appear—the master and two others. A field of three. Master and huntsman confer for a moment, then they wheel and move off through a gateway to go down into a rough combe; I slip through the gate and wait for a little while under the bank.

Winter hind-hunting. It is the hardest of all hunting, making the greatest demands on men and horses, and hounds too, in the worst weathers of the year, often under almost impossible conditions. The winter-hard hinds are as tough as leather, running faster than any stag when they put their minds to it, yet often doubling and twisting amazingly. The horseman must alternatively race or wait soaked and shivering in a biting wind, while hounds must often splash for hours in and out of chilling icy streams. The rivers are swollen and the fords are dangerous. Hinds and even hounds may end by drowning. In former times, I believe, hounds did not hunt in midwinter. Such winter hunting was considered so severe in its effect on both horse and hound that hind-hunting was stopped at Christmas, to be resumed later in the spring with the pursuit of barren hinds. Now, however, hounds hunt all through the season, in all weathers except hard frost and very deep snow.

Even under the bank the wind buffets and snatches. There is nothing to be seen in the wet wood just below. Since hounds did not kennel they must be drawing with the pack somewhere farther down—they must be sure of hinds or one hind on her own in the covert. For a little while I wait hopefully, but the only sound that comes up the wind is an occasional faint thin note of the horn, a long way off, and not coming nearer. So I come back again to the road, resume my thoughts of food, fire and dry warmth, and hurry down the world of fields and farms and friendly folk.

December

In the wood that clings to the hollow shoulder of the hill
there is stillness and silence. The gnarled and twisted oak trees,
their growth distorted between wind and stone, dig their roots
deep into the crevices of the rock, holding themselves as with
knotted fingers to the scanty earth. From their lichen-encrusted
branches long trails of Spanish moss hang like cobwebs,

grey-green, pallid, like dead hands from a ghost world. Underfoot is a world of deep and dripping moss, and fallen rotting branches covered with strange growths and creeping things, all tumbled over rocks slippery as grease and tanged with wet brown bracken. Little rills of water trickle down from hidden springs, spilling moisture all around. On the fringe of the wood the hazels put forth swelling catkins, giving promise of spring and the hope of light and sun.

Below the wood the river curls round the foot of the matted cliff, twisting and looping amongst swampy rush beds and pebble shelves, and faintly its voice comes up to the trees, and to me where I stand in the bracken. Through the lattice of trunks and branches its snake-like course is brightly visible, turning about the big hills beyond rising grey in the falling drizzle.

Now a sudden sound is heard through the wood—the muffled hoof-falls of a horse on the crumbling narrow path above the trees. I see a splash of red, the red coat of a huntsman on a big chestnut—a glorious intense red, moving along the rim of the wood. He looks downwards all the while into the tangle. There they are, the hounds, flickering through the scrub of the precipitous slope, white and tan and black. He calls to them, urging them on, encouraging them, as they quest down the wet wood. They go on down, their sterns waving. The wood swallows them again for a space.

A sudden whimper, a cry, and then a crash of hound-voices from the depths of the hanging wood! How they cry! The music echoes and re-echoes from wall to wall of the valley as they course their fox down to the river's edge. The huntsman rides to the rim of the rocks and stands poised for a moment. Just then the grey rain stops and lifts, and reveals the wide view like a superb backcloth, hill and moor, field and valley. The light strikes the hoary, bearded oaks below and the red coat above. It is an unforgettable picture.

There's a distant holloa from the farm across the river—the fox has crossed, and the hounds are following, swimming now in the racing waters. The huntsman wheels and gallops away, on to the path that leads down to the ford.

From where I stand I can see them emerge on the farther bank, the hounds running up under a long hedge towards the farm. From up the river appear a number of horsemen who have crossed by a higher ford. They go on up the pale green fields, the cry of the hounds still coming across the valley, and then the rain descends again and blots them out. I climb to the top of the wood and go home.

Presently the weather improves and clears away to a fine afternoon, and we set out to recover some trespassing cattle and to mend the fence they have broken down. We descend into the combe where the two streams meet, and cross to collect the beasts from the other side. They are sulky and do not want to come, but finally we persuade them, and they come charging down the steep slope amidst the ochre-dun hill grass and brown bracken. In the bottom they check defiantly for a moment, then plunge into the little river and splash their way over and up the opposite bank with a heave of their great red bodies and a flash of their big white horns. What a fine sight they make as they go thrashing through the water and soft ground, and up the farther rise! I know not what it is, but somehow the sight of cattle on the move always stirs something deep within me—something long forgotten, yet deeply satisfying.

The afternoon is very lovely in the little valley under the steep matted hillsides, and by the fringe of the tangle of woods. Birch and ash and thorn jostle together, and purple sloes cling still to branches hoary and grey-green with lichen, and the silver ash trunks are buttoned with emerald moss. The little brown-and-silver river sings a rippling song beside us, and overhead there are wisps of blue sky showing through rifts of soft cloud. We fell a birch sapling to make posts for the broken fence, and the chips fly from the axe milky-white and fall in a scatter on the grass. For a while we work, setting the posts and hammering them in and straining and nailing fresh wire along the tops. It is a pleasant job, putting up a fence. One feels a sense of con-structiveness and finally of accomplishment, as one looks on the shine of the new wire and posts and sees the baleful looks of the thwarted cattle. A good deal of ingenuity is needed in erecting a fence along a stream bank, for it is not always easy to find firm footing for the posts between rocks in one place and oozing bog in the next—and cattle have an unerring instinct for the weak places in any fence—and one must have a firm strainer-post somewhere to keep the wire taut.

When we have finished, the job is not too badly done, and we can go home with the knowledge of not having wasted our time. We collect our tools and go. I stop for a moment to pick up a few of the birch chips. They have an orange rind between the bark and the milky splinters, and are like painted things. They seem too pretty to cast away so I put them in my pocket. How often it is that one picks up some small thing of nature—a feather, a stone or a mossy twig—and is amazed by the strange beauty inherent in it! Bewildered, too, by all the diversity of shape and colour and texture that is around one in this mortal life, and overwhelmed by all the inexplicable wonder that is the common world, as by a revelation.

§

THE PILE of fresh-quarried stone lies to the side of the yard, propped as it were against the bank, with the sun and the wind licking at it. Stone. Exmoor stone, North Devon stone, the living rock of the land. Great angular blocks harsh and intractable and jag-ended. Blue stone, water-blue in the drying light, darkening to indigo in the shadow. Flames of rust-gold suffusing the blue like a sullen fire, ochre-yellow and brown mingling and deepening to almost wine-red in places. Veins of marble-white creeping thread-like through the masses. Stone—rock indeed. . . . I hardly know how properly to describe it except to say that it seems to be very hard, dense sandstone, shaling in places to slate, yet so hard in others as to be almost a millstone grit. I would make a guess that it came from a quarry just south of the line of the high moor, where the rock is darker and harder than on the northern or eastern side.

There is power in rock, and a deep fascination. One reaches out and touches it and feels the great weight of it, and the hardness and angularity of it, and the sharpness that jags one's hands. It is the bone of the land upon which all things rest and from which all things grow. Here it is the scarp of our combes, the walls of our buildings, the facing of our banks, the posts of our gates, the floors of our yards, the metalling of our roads. Its intractability gives us the form of our dwellings and its availability the long miles of dyking across hill and combe. It is the beginning and the end of all man's handiwork upon the moor.

The land of Exmoor is one great mass of Devonian rock, ancient rock that is a mixture of hard dark sandstones and shaly slates, with here and there a few seams of other sorts of stone for variation. It—the Devonian—has kinship with the Old Red Sandstone of Wales across the channel, and is sometimes so called, though in actual fact it has little resemblance, and red is not its dominant colour.

Our Exmoor stone has as great a range of colouring as of texture, varying according to district and sometimes to strata. It may be silver-grey, blue, rose-pink, red-brown, rusty-ochre, deep plum-colour or dark purple, or blue-black. It may also be streaked or mottled in any colours. As far as locality is concerned the tendency is for the stone to be more reddish on the eastern side of the moor and more blue-grey or rust-streaked to the west. The stone towards Porlock is red, brown or purplish. That over on the Hawkridge and Dulverton side is blue-black flared with ochre. Farther west into Devon it tends to be mingled blue and rust colour. Most of the slates and shales are of a silvery colour. Whatever the original colouring of the rock, though, it all soon weathers together to a pervading dark grey —the grey of the Exmoor walls that look blue in the moorland light.

Surface stone is everywhere abundant on the moor. Scarps and outcrops and clitters of rock are to be found in almost every combe and on every hillside. Even where normally clothed with earth and vegetation, the rock is never very far from the light, excepting only in the region of bogs. Hence from the beginning man has had a plentiful supply of rough building material all around him and ready to hand. When the first farmer settlers threw up the banks of their little fields and set out the foundations of their dwellings they reached out and took what nature provided, and used the raw stone in the way that seemed best suited, and that manner of using has never altered in all the centuries. In turn the stone and its using have moulded and governed the form of all buildings on the moor, shippon and house, wall and bridge and church together, and the wild wind and rain have hammered the rest between them.

Whether soft shale or hard sandstone, the stone of the moor is of one character in that it is all obstinate and intractable, and incapable of being dressed in any way. It must be used always in rubble or ragwork fashion, with thick mortar and an avoidance of elaboration. This sets the style for the long low buildings, thick-walled, plain and severe, no larger than necessary, and often built right into the hillsides, crouching as it were against the wind and wild weather. The latter characteristic, peculiar to the region, and now so frowned upon by modern progressive thought, probably had several virtues to commend it to the original builders. Firstly, flat ground about a site that is neither exposed hilltop nor valley marsh is very rare in this land of hills, and since one must therefore build on a slope, the obvious and most simple thing to do is to hollow out the desired space cavewise and build the edifice within. Secondly, the process of excavation would automatically produce a good deal of loose building-stone, which would reduce the labour of stone-hauling for the actual walls even less. Thirdly, and most vital of all, by the setting of the building right into the hill a degree of warmth and shelter would be obtained that could not be gained by any other means. And on this last I can speak from personal experience, for over a period of many years I have lived in a succession of such dwellings, each built so that it was set right into the hillside, with its face to the sun and its back roof almost touching the earth; and in every case the place was cool in summer and so warm and cosy in the winter that the rooms struck warm to one even on the coldest day and when there had been no fire in the house for a while. There was never any wind or draught, the south front was always a suntrap, and each little place extremely comfortable to live in. Was it not damp, you will ask? The answer is, strangely enough, no, not more than is any house in this wet west country. The modern ruling about a dwelling-house having perforce a three-foot clearance from the surrounding ground is absolute rubbish, and proves our ancestors to have been a good deal wiser than we in this one respect at least.

Be it as it may, both house and shippon were built on this burrowing principle on almost every farm between West Somerset and North Devon. Another fallacy is the prevailing idea that for healthy and comfortable living a ceiling height of not less than eight or nine feet is necessary. In most parts the average height of a cottage ceiling is six feet six inches and this gives ample head clearance to all but a giant and makes for conservation of warmth in winter.

I walk on; the day is all bright sunshine and blue sky, with a fresh west wind blowing a few clouds, indigo and peach-gold, up from the rim of the Forest. Suddenly there is the perfect arc of a rainbow hung in the clear sky to the north. It is brilliant, a perfect arch of colour, with only its western foot in the rising cloud. For a moment the landscape glows a fierce gold; then the horizon of the Forest turns to a line of blue-black, and the first scattering of a shower falls from somewhere and I run for shelter.

This phenomenon, a rainbow in a clear blue sky, I have seen before in the hills, even on a day when there were no showers and only the slightest wisp of cloud about. I do not know the cause of its appearance under such conditions or whether it is to be observed in other parts, but can only say that I have remarked it several times.

The sun sinks tonight amidst a great cloudscape of tattered and tumbling clouds flying before the wind, dark and gold-topped in a brittle sky. Just about sunset the clouds begin to tower amazingly. One cloud on the west rears right up like a vast pillar, a fantastic shape in the space of the heavens, like a prophetic portent speaking in an unknown tongue, then sinks back spent into the wrack, bowed before the sunset light. Like music the light and the great forms die away, and the scene is finished.

§

MIST AND rain and black wet heather—and nothing else. I eat the remains of my lunch with cold stiff fingers, and decide that I have had enough of the moor for one day, after a fruitless morning looking for hounds on the hill. For just a moment the mist lifts a little, revealing the hill for a space before it begins to close in again. The moorland stretches away to meet the infinity of the mist, lying all around one in dark and sombre majesty, a waste of old heather and sear grass, and twisted thorn trees like witches—a primal landscape all black and umber and ochre and touched with russet.

But home is a welcome place at the end of such a day, and I hurry down from the hill with thoughts of food and a fire to speed me. Dusk and the mist merge together as I reach the gate and the door, and good is the blaze on the hearth within!

Now I sit before the fire again, and look around my room and remember past things, and muse on this and that and watch the burning wood. The firelight flickers about the room, filling it with orange warmth as a cave is filled, setting the shadows dancing over the floor and on the walls and in the corners. The lamp is not yet lit; the fire holds kingdom from the fireplace and is light and heat and company all in one against the winter night.

On the walls the antlers hang; three heads, and their shadows move on the smooth plaster like the branches of trees in the wind. Three good heads, a twelve-pointer and two tens. Like our ancestors of a thousand years ago we still bring home the red deer antlers—trophies of the chase and spoils of the wood— and hang them on our walls or nail them to the gables, and on winter evenings remember the sport of the summer.

This is the country of the deer, and everywhere you will find the antlers of the lordly stag set up in pride. There is scarcely a dwelling anywhere on or about Exmoor that has not a head displayed somewhere, and often there are several to be seen at once. On walls inside and out, over fireplaces, above windows and doors, set on gables and posts, you will see them—great heads, small heads, fine ones, indifferent ones, heads that are odd and heads that are strangely deformed. The variety is infinite, for no two heads are ever quite alike. They have the individuality of all living natural things, and are of endless interest to those who care for such.

What makes a fine head? A compound of several things, I would say—number of points, evenness, form, size and weight or substance. A stag's head should have, firstly, strong powerful beams which should be of good length, and which should curve upwards and outwards in a wide satisfying spread. Secondly, he should have 'all his rights', which is to say the brow, bay and trey points or tines, and these should all be long and bold, especially the brow-tines. Thirdly, he should carry two, three or more points at the top of each antler, and these should likewise be long and distinct and also well spread apart. Fourthly, both antlers must be even, that is to say balanced and symmetrical in form or shape, with the number of points the same on both sides. In addition to all this it is considered desirable that the antler should be dark in colour and rough in texture, only the tips of the points being smooth and white. Incidentally, Exmoor antlers are always referred to as a 'head,' although the almost universal method of mounting is that of simply cutting out the top of the skull and setting it upon a shield of wood. A full taxidermist head is not usual in these parts.

In assessing a head one must always bear in mind the growth-cycle of the antlers and the years of a stag. The antlers of the red deer are shed every spring and a completely new growth put forth in the space of about three months. Generally speaking it may be said that each new growth attains a larger and heavier size than the one preceding it, so that with every year of a stag's life the head increases in dimension and in the number of points. In his first year after calf hood a young male deer throws two small points; in his second a longer spire or upright; and in the third an upright with brow and trey. Thereafter his head increases by bay point and two atop, and so perhaps to three, four or even more atop. A general increase may go on until his powers wane with old age, and then his head will probably 'go back' and become poorer and imperfect towards his end. A big old stag, still in his full vigour, and not yet failing, may throw a magnificent head of eighteen points, or even more. Such a head will usually be palmated at the tops, the points held as though on outstretched hands.

With regard to size for age, though, it must be remembered that feeding is a great factor. A stag that has fed well on lush ground will throw a bigger head, and at an earlier age, than will one that has had only poor, sparse grazing.

Various peculiarities occur from time to time. One comes across heads malformed with bent or twisted antlers, or heads that are one-horned, or those of nott-stags which never threw more than a knob of antler in all their lives. Even normal antlers are often far from perfect, a point present on one side being absent on the other, or both bay points or even brows may be missing. It is hard to account for these things, but I have heard it said that an injury to the horn while it is in the velvet may be a cause of malformation.

The head of the average wild Exmoor stag is, I should say, finer and heavier than the head of the average Highland stag, though perhaps I am not competent to judge, for I have seen far more Exmoor heads than Scottish ones. Anyway the great Ensleigh Head, the greatest wild deer head seen in Britain in this century, was almost certainly that of a roving Exmoor stag. This mighty head, recovered in Cornwall in 1951 (I think), bore twenty points and may have had twenty-four a few years before when the splendid beast was in his prime. Two locally famous heads are the Haddon Stag (a great twelve-pointer) and the St Audries Head (a massive fourteen-pointer), both taken by the Devon and Somerset Staghounds in the last century. There are many more almost or equally as good. The finest array of Exmoor heads to be seen anywhere, and probably the best collection of wild-deer antlers in the country, is that displayed at the Exford kennels of the Devon and Somerset Staghounds. There are also three splendid heads hung in the Exford Memorial Hall. The biggest head I ever saw alive was that of the great stag run from West Molland to Winsford in the season of 1959. All his rights, and five and seven on the big palmated tops—an eighteen-pointer.

In the north, I believe, an even twelve-point head is called a 'Royal', but I have never heard that term used in the West Country.

§

A DAWN wind, like a benediction, sweet and strong, bringing all the scent of the moor and the sea over the hedges and into the fields. A little early sunshine and patches of blue sky looking through the moving sou'west clouds, and the sheep lying in a garland across the big field, just raising their heads at the sound of footsteps in the morning light. A moorland Christmas—Christmas Day in the morning.

From out of space the strains of *Adeste Fideles* come clear on the wind, coming from a distant wireless set by an open door, and the sheep themselves seem like a Christmas carol as they look up from the grass. Robins trill from the hedges as I pass and cows low from the shippons in the yard, and somewhere a cock crows to add his voice to the sounds of early morning. A green Christmas, and we are glad to see it.

Away over the fields the little moorland church beyond the hill waits for its worshippers from afar. Soon its bells will ring, and its folk will come, a few on foot, but most in cars and Land-rovers, for the hill country parish is wide and scattered. I think of it now, and remember its small squat tower of rough grey stone, with the ferns that have come to roost in the crannies, inside as well as out, green fingers above the bell-ropes. I remember the narrow nave, and the chancel decked with holly, and the steps down from the door with the big wide view of the heather-dark moor and the woods in the valley below. Little grey church—it has sat a long time on its hillside in the sun and the wind since first its stones were raised, and forgotten hands set the round Norman arch above the open door. Last night it was lit with lamps and candles; this morning the sun shines through its coloured glass and soon there will be singing again under the timbered roof. Once more men will come to listen to a story told again and again, and to remember in their hearts an older rejoicing in the triumph of light over darkness.

Christmas Day on a hill farm differs not in any material way from any other day, save that a few folk may try to get down to the church for the morning service. The beasts must be fed and tended and the sheep looked to as usual, and all the heavy yard work done and all the innumerable odd chores accomplished. The midday meal is usually a scratch one, for the Christmas dinner is put back to the evening so that all can eat in peace after the last of the day's tasks are done and the beasts bedded down for the night.

The days of Christmas are short and the nights long, but they are seldom really cold. One does not look for snow and hard weather until after New Year. December is usually an open month and a green Christmas the rule. Only once do I remember a white Christmas when it snowed in the morning and turned to a blizzard in the afternoon, and the cattle came back into the shippons covered with white like the ornaments on a Christmas cake. But snow, despite its beauty and though it may represent the traditional image of Christmas, is a thing no one desires to see in the hills until one must. It is the green winter that is always hoped for, despite its disadvantages.

So the day's work goes on until it is time again to see to the sheep. Dusk comes quickly on the heels of the short afternoon, and I take my staff and step out quickly for the top fields. Westward, the last rays of the setting sun pierce the cloud in glory like the light from an altar. In the flaming light I lift my eyes and look up at the five great hills that raise their heads all around, barrow-crowned every one. Many are the nameless ones whose spirits must brood over the heights where once in life they hunted and fought and lusted, and where now their ashes sleep in the earth. This night we keep their festival and ours, the turning of the year, the rising of the sun, the step from darkness into light, life and hope and the promise of all things made new. Strange that the Christian birth should be one with the ancient festival of resurgent life. Or perhaps not so strange.

And now it is dusk, and all the beasts are fed and settled for the night, the sheep in the field, the cows in the shippon, the horses in the stable. The lights glow in the house, there is bustle in the kitchen, an undercurrent of anticipation—and at last we sit down to our long-awaited dinner. A mighty feast it is, with a turkey so big that it will hardly go on the largest dish for the centre-piece, and so many things else that we can barely consume them all. A merry Christmas to us all, and many more to come!

Late at night I rise from the fire, and take a turn around the yard, and with lantern in hand look into those buildings where beasts are tied, making sure all is well. The light throws monstrous shadows from the dozing beasts on to the rough walls behind. In the last shippon, that next to the stable, a huge figure stands against the wall, almost touching the low ceiling. It is our great red bull, and as he turns his ponderous head, sleepy-eyed, the light catches at his thick white horns. Beside him two cows lie at rest, and by his head a small calf sleeps. The light and shadow moulds them, making of them a sculptured group, and they seem without time, as though they had always been like that. They are figures from a manger scene, living counterparts of those small images set forth in wood last night within the crib in the bright lamp-lit church. A happy

Christmas to you, beasts in the straw, for perhaps you know more than we do on this Christmas night.

§

SUN AND frost and a clear winter sky. How lovely, how joyful, is a fine bright day in the midst of winter—a doorway of brilliance between the opening and closing of a year! Sharp white frost under a sky of duck-egg blue, and a sun rising in golden radiance from behind the hedges to light the silvery world, and not one breath of wind to stir the sweet, sharp morning air. The grass underfoot is stiff and rustling, and the white rime lies on the fields and the sheep have frost on their backs, and as they get up they leave green patches on the grass where their warm bodies have rested all night. The scent of the frosted grass rises up as the creatures move to and fro, trampling it, and the scent is exquisite, like the very spirit of the earth let loose. Along the hedges, where the spent grasses are tall, the hoarfrost has frozen on the head of each one, turning it to a flower-like spire, and the hedge above glitters and sparkles in the light of the mounting sun.

Slowly, gradually, the sun rises, dispelling the hoarfrost and breathing along the banks with a spring-like warmth. The gorse bushes in the hollows have already put forth a few first yellow flowers, and one can just catch their sweet fragrance, like a whisper from a far-away land. Out across the big field a great flock of lapwings are busy about their business of life, settling and shifting and rising and settling again, with plaintive, mournful cries, flaunting their black-rimmed wings against the sky.

Over the moor and over the distant fields is my way, to a farm on the edge of the Forest, to see the hare-hounds hunt this morning on the hills above the narrow Exe. The midday sun has climbed the sky by the time I turn into the yard under tall bare beeches and join the company of other country folk, all chattering and cheerful, partaking of cake and other refreshment about the door of the house. A battered van backs down the lane and into the space, and someone resplendent in a green jacket undoes the door and lets forth the small excited pack. How little they seem, these small basset-hounds, after the tall, upstanding foxhounds and staghounds. Yet what they lack in size they make up in liveliness, and if enthusiasm stands for anything, they promise good sport.

The courtesies of the day done, the hounds move off. Sterns up, the eager little pack trots off between amateur huntsman and honorary whippers-in, and the field, some score strong, follows out of the yard and down the lane with a scuffled treading of boots. They turn up across a couple of fields, and out through a gate to the tawny moor, into the space of sedge and rush and the arching empty sky. Over the rise and down a little way, and the bottle-green jackets are bright in the winter sun, vivid colour amongst the knee-deep rush. They throw off across the rushy ground and cast this way and that, going on down and out of sight, whilst the rest of us move along the top of the ridge. For a while there is nothing, no sound, and only an occasional flicker of movement from below. The minutes slip by, and perhaps half an hour, and then there's a whimpering cry that grows to a chorus, and there goes the hare, fresh from her form, and here come the hounds, running like furies and crying like banshees. Along the hill and into a combe that is a deep hollow cleft in the scarp, and oh, the ring of their voices that echo from wall to wall in the depths—clear, rich, melodious, full and bell-like, such a singing that is worthy of the great hounds of old, out of all keeping with the small stature of the singers. Now they are out of the combe and away again. Running and scrambling, we try to hold them in view, splashing across sogging ground, tumbling over jagged stone walls, clambering through wind-battered hedges, but for all our striving and lack of care for our limbs and clothing, they outdistance us fast, and we are left in silence again.

Yet after a while they come round in a circle again, and again we stand and watch them in the rush beds on the hill. They are silent now, for puss has eluded them. To and fro, they try every hollow under the rushes, and every clump of sedge. Persistent they strive to find the place where she has clapped down. They draw together in the deepest rush, and suddenly up she jumps right in the midst of them! Like an eel she twists and leaps and evades their charging rush, and out from the ring of them she

175

goes bounding over the tussocks to liberty, while 'even the ranks of Tuscany could scarce forbear to cheer'.

The little hounds run another circle, and after a while yet another—it would seem that a hare prefers to run a ring, seldom getting more than a mile away from the form where she was found—but not getting near to their quarry again. There are fresh hares about to complicate matters, and so at last we all go home, bloodless, satisfied enough with the afternoon's vigorous exercise and the day in the open air.

The short day is already closing as I start my long walk home, and half way I turn aside for a talk with friends at a farm under the hill and am persuaded to stay for a while, and to supper; and so time is set back for me even more. It is very late by the time I reach the first of our fields.

Now I walk home alone, up over the old pack-horse track, just before midnight. No moon, but the stars are so brilliant that I am able to pick my way up the rough track without recourse to a torch. New Year's Eve. I walk slowly across the top fields and then stand for a while, gazing up at the stars, reluctant to leave the beauty of the night. The stars blaze in a velvet sky, more brilliant than I have ever seen them in England before, or so it seems. Each one is a pinpoint of glittering white light. Seen through the tops of the tall beech hedge they seem as though snared in a net. How wonderful are all things—heaven and earth, and all creation between. A moment spent in prayer, and then I turn through the gate to home.

January

A CLEAR bright winter morning, and all is ready for the baling of the big Nine Acres hayrick. Hay in January—and an almost perfect summer-like day. Bright blue sky, flecked with just a few floating white clouds, a clear golden landscape and a light westerly wind, cold but fresh. Far away Dunkery Beacon lies like a sleeping lion on the horizon, dark-maned and tawny-flanked with shadow and sun.

Now the noise of the blue tractor dragging the baler up to Nine Acres. Extra hands arriving for the job. Then another tractor with a big trailer. The chug-chug of machinery starting into life. Now on to the rick with pitchforks, and to work.

It is hot work on the tight-pressed rick—the hay is very solid and hard to undo. Steady work from early morning to dusk, feeding the baler as though into the mouth of an endlessly hungry monster, forking, loosening, heaving, pitching, until one sweats as though it were truly summer. All the while the strong sweet scent of the hay mingles with the aromatic smell of the men's cigarettes, strong and heady, almost overpowering, intensified by its six-month concentration in the big rick. The rhythmic throbbing and clanking of the machinery makes an endless chain of sound. Out in the field a great growing pile of pale golden bales builds up wall-like on the grass despite the constant coming and going of the tractor-and-trailer taking them home to the barn.

Now a break, and lunch in the field, half an hour sitting in the pale winter sunshine in the shelter of the rick, eating and talking. Sandwiches, cakes and hot tea in flasks. Hay tea in January! The dogs are overjoyed.

All too soon the lunch-time pool of silence is broken by the restarting chug and throb as the work begins again. On to the rick once more with sleeves rolled up. It seems as though we shall never come to the bottom of the rick—it is so solid that with all our work it does not seem to diminish. The sun wanes and still we fork on. But at last, at long last, we strike the staddle of the base. It is finished! The tractor stops, and the baler clanks to a standstill.

The last load of bales goes home. The sun has set and we gather up our coats and forks and go too. The field is empty and silent, and alone in the twilight the baler stands against the pale sky like a monster sunk into sleep.

As we come home the winter night is full of the sweet smell of hay on the chilling air, and a bright half-moon hangs suspended in the sky. One will sleep tonight with a greater sense of security for knowing that the barns and tallets are stuffed full with the good hay, for winter is before us, and all too quickly this fair open weather can turn to frost and snow, and to long, hard, hungry weeks with many mouths to feed before the spring.

THE CRY of the hounds comes over the moor and up from the valley, borne on the cold north wind, and all one's senses are kindled and quickened. They are in the wood now, where the two little rivers meet, and their voices echo from side to side of the brake. They are coming nearer, and I hear a holloa not far away.

Suddenly she comes, the brown hind, up from the wood and the combe below, running along the line of a high beech hedge. She runs with the rocking gait of her kind, not fast, not slow, but with the tireless stride of the wild red deer. Her lean body is dark with sweat and the rough winter coat. Her slender head is held high on the long snake neck, and the long ears are laid down and back. Yet tired she must be, for already she has ringed and circled for ten miles or more this morning.

Now the hounds come, not very far behind, running the line in single file, as is the manner of staghounds, every nose on the scent. They give tongue, but intermittently, for the running is hard. The ground shakes as the first horsemen come, pounding through the heather, and a red coat flashes in the winter sun.

She goes for the high moor now, up to the sedge and the wind-bleached bent and the wet black bog, straight as an arrow now, by the barrow sunk in the rushes, and over the hill where the shag-coated ponies bunch and wheel. Through the little plantation of stunted pine that offers no harbour, over the track that leads to the lonely farm, over the heather where the blue stones hide, and down the combe that leads to the big wide river that clatters to the ancient five-arched bridge, and her head is set for the desolate Forest hills.

Up the long river valley she turns, where rush and reed and uneasy ground meet the twisting, running river, and the wet rock breaks up through the frothing water. The horses are beat —all but a few. The blue shadows draw down the hills and the valley is sunless under their walls. Only the huntsman's voice comes up from the hollowness.

The hounds come slowly on the rough and soggy ground. Scent is difficult and the sun is sinking. Yet she cannot be far in front, and she is tiring. The huntsman rides above the river bank, his red coat bright in the tawny landscape, calling on the hounds to try and sounding thin notes on the horn.

There's a holloa for a view—she is in the water and going on up out of sight. A cry of hound-voices comes down the wind as she leaves the water and they fresh-find. Surely they must take her now. But no—still she goes on, on into the dusk and the Forest hills, with the hounds struggling on the scent. Another ten miles more she will go before they take her in the Bray in the dark tonight.

Thirty miles as hounds ran, they say as they come home in the moonlight over the frosty roads and tracks. A day to be remembered and a run that will stand by any in the annals of hunting.

§

COLD GREY days and bitter winds, and black frosts that set hard in the earth. Now winter has set its teeth in the land, and for the week past an ominous leaden sky has pressed down on field and moor, and all life has shrunk into itself under the stiffening cold. The fields stretch dun-colour under the heavy grey sky, brushed grey-white with frost; and dry white ice lies in the gateways, sharp and splintering in the iron hoof-holes. The bitter north-east wind pierces like a knife-blade, shrivelling all vegetation, licking the moisture out of everything and giving the ground a dry brushed look, seeking out all the chinks in the armour of one's clothing, and biting at one's nose, ears and fingers. A blue-grey fog of coldness lies over the hills, cheerless and drawing dawn and dusk together without any noonday brightness, and in the house one needs a light all day. The hedges stand stark and black, and the sheep, weather-wise, huddle close under them, even climbing half way up the banks to press tight into the hollows. The only volatile life is that of the starlings, who come sweeping low over the hedges in huge flocks with a great rushing sound, or rise from the grass with a noise like a thunderclap.

Now all sheep are brought down from the top fields and turned into the meadows nearer to home, or over on the south sides of the hills. For soon it must snow, and woe betide the farmer who has neglected to move his flock from the places where the deep white drifts will pile up under the wind and the big high hedges. Now one looks to one's stores and is glad that the barns and tallets are full, and that the beasts are in the shippons, the horses in the stable and the log-pile big by the saw-bench shed.

And now, before the onset of midwinter, is the time of pig-killing. This morning the back kitchen has had its ritual scrubbing out, and the copper set going with seething hot water in the cauldron and wood smoke like incense rising from the fire beneath. Now our neighbour arrives to do the deed, and by concerted effort the fat pig is hauled protesting from her sty to the place of execution by the kitchen doorstep. A cord is wound round her upper jaw to hold her head steady, and then at once she is stunned by the humane killer. Quickly the man sticks her with a sharp knife as she goes down, cutting open her throat from chin to gullet, so that the blood gushes out, pumped by the death throes of the thrashing limbs, pouring out a great red stream over the back-kitchen floor, down the steps, and far out into the yard in a long crimson stain. At last she lies still, smeared all over with blood and her throat gaping like a red-covered book turned inside-out. Sixteen score of pork, ham and bacon. Alas, poor pig, with what delicious dreams of roasts and fries and pies and brawns and delicacies untold we view her carcass! She is so heavy that two strong men cannot lift her, but at last by some manœuvring and concerted effort we manage to get her on to the 'ladder', and she lies in state.

Now come the scalding and scrubbing of the carcass, and the gutting and preliminary cutting up. All the cats and dogs gather and hang round, expectant, no doubt like us dreaming of visionary feasts. There will be liver for supper tonight, and fried kidney for breakfast and tongue for tomorrow's tea, and pig's head brawn after that. The day after tomorrow, when the carcass has been dismembered and properly cut up, we shall have roast pork, hot or cold, every day for a fortnight, and then bacon for the rest of the year, and one ham for shearing and the other for next Christmas.

After an afternoon's labours the great white carcass hangs in splendour on the pulley-hook, high enough to be out of reach of four-footed marauders while waiting for the morrow, and we turn again to all the usual tasks that must be done. Presently the engine begins to chug and the buzz-saw to whine, and I go to lend a hand with the sawing. The big beech-poles are heavy with frozen sap, and the frost in them bites one's hands with numbing cold. The big toothed wheel screeches through the icy timber, and after a while a heap of logs piles up beside the bench, promising fire and flames on the hearth tonight. What a wonderful thing is timber! It is fuel for the fire, and wood for the roof and fence and door, and the makings of tools and furnishings as well. We make good use of most of our local wood. Beech has little constructional value, but there is no better fuel. Like the ash it will burn green, and indeed burns much better so with the sap in it, than it does when dry. It burns with both brilliance and lasting power, and is good equally on an open hearth or in a modern stove. Ash is too valuable to burn in these parts, as it has a greater use as poles for fencing, etc., and as stall-trees for the cow-ties, and also for the renewing of tool handles. Oak is the stuff of gate-posts, and what is left over makes good backstick for the fire. Sallow and birch can both be used for posts when ash is not available, and both will burn well enough, though sallow is awkward to saw. Thorn burns with a very fierce heat. Gorse makes the greatest blaze of all, fierce, hot and brilliant, but few folk faggot gorse any more. It is many years since I saw a faggot-rick in a yard.

The desolation of dusk settles on the cold land. One hurries about the last chores of the day to keep warm, and thinks kindly and with longing of the fire and the hot meal to come. There is an emptiness about the cold like the void of space. The fields sink into the nothingness of night. Somewhere, far away, the dragon's eyes of a car on the distant road make a momentary glow of light in the gloom, and then all is darkness again. The short day is gone, and there is only the blackness of a January night.

§

SNOW. It has come at last, deep snow, white and foreboding, to close the days of January. It came last night, at first falling steadily, silent, unhurrying, covering all the ground with a thick soft mantling and all the trees with ghostly white, then turning suddenly on a rising wind to a blinding blizzard. I remember battling my way home across the fields in the dark, in the teeth of the blizzard, with the snow whirling round me and all deep and muffling underfoot. Like a journey to the ends of the earth.

And now the world is snowbound, transfigured into another creation, unlike that to which our eyes are accustomed. The sky is iron dark, the earth white, muffled in a blanket through which the streams thread snakewise, dark and lipped with ice. The trees and hedges are loaded with a white burden as much as their branches can bear, and the farm buildings sit black and crouching under their hoods of snow. Long drifts lie under the hedges and across the gateways, curved and sculptured by eddies of wind into strange shapes and solid, arrested waves. Everything now is noiseless and still, and one's boots move with a floundering tread.

It is well that the sheep were brought down from the top fields two days ago and the flocks moved over to the south side of the hill, else we would be digging them out of the drifts this morning. Even so they must be fed. I shoulder the heavy bale of hay and struggle up the lane for a quarter of a mile. The sheep hear or smell me coming from afar, and bunch against the field gate in a seething, bleating mass. They mob me as I struggle through the gate, almost sweeping me off my feet, and tear at the corners of the bale as I throw it down. At last I manage to cut the strings and throw it wide, and they fall upon it, battling for the shreds of hay like ravening wolves. Gone are all the traditional docility and natural shyness—hunger drives out all instincts but that for food. Poor beasts, one bale seems little enough among a hundred-odd.

January snow in the hills. We receive it philosophically but not without foreboding. It is the noon of winter, and snow may lie long. We hope it will only be for a week perhaps, or less, but we cannot be sure that it will not last for three months or more. The great snow of 1947 came in about the middle of January and did not go until April. Then the moor was buried so deep in frozen snow that one could walk over the hedges on the top of it, and be lost for lack of landmarks. That year the sheep died in hundreds, and in some parts cattle and ponies too.

Mercifully such a winter is rare, and in general nine out of ten Exmoor winters are mild in comparison with those of the eastern parts of the country. The severity of an average moorland winter is to be measured in terms of battering wind and rain rather than snow and frost. But nevertheless snow when it comes is always ominous.

The narrow lanes choke quickly with the snow, and the wind blows deep drifts into the hollow gateways. The lonely farms are quickly cut off, and then each must battle with its own troubles in its own isolation. If the snow lies long and the preceding harvest season has been bad, the spectre of starvation walks above the beasts. No matter how foresighted one may have been in the matter of laying in feeding stuffs, there is never enough in a really bad winter in this pastoral country. Things are much better now than they used to be with the present long-distance transport of essential foodstuffs, snow-ploughs to keep the top roads open, and powerful tractors to hand. But none the less a hard winter is still bad enough.

About the yards the snow is soon churned to brown and dirty slush by all the coming and going between barn and shippon and by the hoofs of the beasts turned out to drink at the splat. The shippons are cleaned as hastily as possible while the inmates are at water, so that the cattle may not stand for long in the icy air, and the bales of heavy hay and the yellow oaten sheaves are broken in the low mangers for their return. Yet it is nearly a day's work in the short winter light before all is done for the beasts about the yard and the horses in the stable, and the pressing dusk of the afternoon tells one that it is time to tend the sheep again.

Again one turns into the blankness of the snow, past the hens that huddle stupefied around the open doors of their houses, and out to the land and the fields, lifting one's eyes as one does to the white-backed, empty hills under the iron sky of dusk. Where are the ponies now, I wonder? Somewhere down in some south-facing, north-sheltered combe, tails to the wind. It is seldom they come to any harm. The little horses will survive where sheep and cattle perish, delving in the snow with their forefeet in search of food, and mouthing the whiteness for drink. The moor farmers say that the proof of a pony's breeding is whether it can survive, without any feeding or aid from man, a hard winter on the hill. The true Exmoor succumbs rarely to the hardships of nature, though half-bred stock may suffer much under severe conditions.

Yet once a herd of good ponies did die in the snow, on Withypool Hill. I have heard it told that in a great blizzard of the 1880's a group of ponies took shelter in the corner of the moor where the big hedges of Brightworthy and Knighton come together, and that there the drifting snow built a great wall around them, so that they were shut in, and there they perished. One pony only was able to break away, a stallion the property of the Miltons of Withypool, 'the best horse on the hill', and he fought his way out and down to Landacre Bridge. But he had a very long tail, and as he went the snow balled up on the trailing hair, bigger and bigger, until it became a huge frozen block, and the weight of it dragged him down so that at last he, too, dropped and died exhausted in the snow. When the body was found, with its great block of ice, old Mr Milton said that at least this should never happen again, and so at the next drift he cut the long tails of all his ponies. And that, so they say, is why the Withypool ponies all have their tails squared off every year.

At last the sheep are finished with, and I can turn for home, across the unfamiliar land. Snow seems to give the countryside a new aspect and oneself another vision. One sees revealed new contours of land, spinneys of trees unguessed at in distant hollows, and one marks the dark curves of big beech hedges anew. The eye is assailed by forms and depths in a familiar scene of which one has not been formerly aware. There is a timelessness in this strange new world on which the hand of man seems to rest but shortly and precariously. The farm buildings huddle close around the house, and the farm itself is an island of humanity in the cold and dark of nature—light and life where the elemental cold freezes blood and sinew. Two people near the farm, moving in the snow, sharp black against the white, are figures from Breughel, and the whole is as a scene from a medieval painting.

How glad one is to come home, and to have a home to return to, on this winter's night. How thankful is one, with the suddenness of a revelation, for the simple elementary blessings of human life—of shelter and food and fire, warmth and comfort and security, and the company of friends—how thankful indeed for all those things which in the ordinary way one takes for granted, and which now, seen and felt against the might of a relentless natural order, assume their true and lasting values.

§

Sun after snow. The morning sun shining on all the whole white expanse from the arc of a pale, clear, cloudless sky.

All around the frozen snow sparkles with endless diamond points of light, and every hedge and tree is bowed with white as though laden with exotic blossom. The hills lie white-gold under the sky of brittle blue, shadowed with turquoise and cobalt in every combe. The light itself seems a new dimension. Beside me a little tree holds fantastic flowers of snow against the deeper blue of the zenith, as though every twig bore a great white magnolia. It is like a new heaven and a new earth.

One's whole being exalts and rejoices, delighting in all the light and space and sense of freedom. Forgotten for a moment is all the hardship of winter and all its work and bitter cold. One feels a desire to shout like a child. For a moment everything is a delight to the senses. One stands in the midst of an eternal now, and time has no meaning.

Yet life must go on, and does go on. The sheep move about the snowbound fields as they wait for food, their criss-cross tracks etched in blue upon the shining surface. Fresh molehills thrust up looking like black hats in the snow. About the farm the day's work goes on as always, with all the endless round of feeding, cleaning out and feeding again, and the middens grow bigger and higher. Icicles like dragon's teeth hang from the shippon roof in a giant fringe, ever increasing in length. Many birds flutter around the yards in search of what they can find. One strange white pigeon perches on the shippon roof, comes down amongst the other birds for a little, then flies away into the trees like a lost spirit. The afternoon wanes and the sun begins to sink in a flaring orange sunset.

Again the day draws to a close. The beasts are fed, the lamps lit, the evening chores done. A cold moon shines on the white roofs. Again we sit by the fire, watching the leaping flames.

Tomorrow it will be February, and the day after that Candlemass Day. Midwinter, and half our winter yet to come. 'Till Candlemass Day keep half your hay.' How true that is here in the hills.

Once more one's thoughts are drawn irresistibly to the moor and the hills. Out beyond our circle of light and warmth, beyond the holding of hedge and field, under the mantle of snow, the moor broods in primeval loneliness, indifferent to man and his cares, concerned only with its own wilderness and the perpetuation of its own kingdom. Out in the night it lies as it has lain for a thousand years and for untold centuries before, holding within itself all the memories of winter and summer, daylight and darkness, sun and moon and stars, of man and beast and strange gods, of all that is past, is present, and is to come.

Note

OF THE various local words or names used, one or two perhaps need some explanation. The term 'splat' is used to denote a little channel of fresh water, guttered down from a spring to supply the needs of a farm or homestead, but 'splat' or 'plat' can also mean any small enclosure of ground—e.g. 'ricksplat', the little enclosure where the corn-ricks are always built. The term 'goyle' ('goyal' or 'goile') is supposed properly to indicate a small dry rift, but we apply it generally to any small combe in the side of a hill. A 'tallet' is in general a loft above a shippon or stable, though specifically it should apply only to one having a stone stairway; a 'linhay' (pronounced linny) is an open-fronted building, and a 'shippon' any place not precisely a linhay, barn or stable, though properly a place for cattle.

In describing plants and flowers I use those common names by which I have always known them, but where a precise identification seems needed I have added the generally accepted Latin name, bearing in mind that local nomenclature often varies considerably in different parts of the country. Bracken is usually called 'fern' here in the hill country.

In those pages descriptive of peat and peat-cutting I stated that I have seen no peat-working anywhere on Exmoor for the past ten years. Since writing this, however, I have come across fresh peat-diggings in the neighbourhood of Exe Head. The method of cutting, I observed, was by means of a trench some two or three feet wide and about three feet deep, and running for many yards across the sedgy ground. The peat-face was black and pure from just under the spine to the depths of the trench, and the bottom was still black and oozing—thrusting down with my stick I could find nothing solid. The turves, laid on the spine to dry, were themselves as hard and black as coal.